University Of Minnesota™
Football Vault™

The History Of The Golden Gophers™

Rick Moore

University of Minnesota™ *FOOTBALL VAULT*™

The History of the Golden Gophers™

Excluding certain works, whose copyright may or may not be noted, ©2008 Whitman Publishing, LLC
3101 Clairmont Road · Suite C · Atlanta GA 30329

Correspondence concerning this book may be directed to the publisher, at the address above.

ISBN: 0794824331
Printed and assembled in China

Note: All removable documents and memorabilia in this book are replicas and not originals themselves.

For a catalog of collectibles-related books, supplies and storage products, visit Whitman Publishing online at **www.whitmanbooks.com**.
For sports books, visit **www.collegevaultbooks.com**.

TABLE OF CONTENTS

REMEMBER THE HISTORY AND TRADITION

Being the head coach of one of the most storied football programs in America is a tremendous responsibility. Not only is it an honor to coach at the University of Minnesota, it is important that people remember the history and tradition of the Golden Gophers, which comes alive in Rick Moore's *University of Minnesota™ Football Vault™: The History of the Golden Gophers.™*

Some of the greatest men ever to coach or play football donned maroon and gold. They include people like Bernie Bierman and Murray Warmath with six national championships between them, Bobby Bell, Bud Grant, Bronko Nagurski and Carl Eller. Their legacy will be forever embedded in Gopher history.

I am more excited today than the day I was hired about the direction of the Golden Gophers football program. Each day is a chance to teach young men about a sport I love, and I am able to share my passion with my staff and players. As the great Tony Dungy said, "I want to win a championship with championship-caliber people!"

Above all else, we will win games with character and class, and we will succeed in the classroom. Gopher football players will not only learn the sport, but they will learn how to become excellent people. This will be a team that the state of Minnesota can celebrate.

We all look forward to the football season, and autumn Saturdays at Minnesota are going to be truly magical beginning Sept. 12, 2009, when TCF Bank Stadium opens its gates for the first time. The game-day rituals will be back again, with the band marching down University Avenue, the team Victory Walk into the stadium, tailgating and fans cheering their Gophers on to victory. People will be able to feel the excitement in the crisp fall air, and these will be the days that dreams are made of because football will be back on campus where it should be.

Football is a sport that can make champions out of its players, and it is my dream to take the Golden Gophers to the Rose Bowl. With the support of the state and its people, the University of Minnesota football team will accomplish more than that. It will bring pride and recognition back to the Gopher greats, as well as to the new gridiron heroes who have yet to be made.

Big Ten champions, Rose Bowl champions and national champions are all titles within our reach. It starts with a belief in the team, coaches and program, and it will blossom into a reality. Minnesota is host to the one of the greatest universities in the country, and as the head football coach, I am honored to be able to lead this program back to the championship level on which it belongs.

Tim Brewster

— Tim Brewster
Head football coach

PILLY, PUDGE AND THE YELL LEADERS

1882-1899

RECORD: 59 WINS, 27 LOSSES, 4 TIES

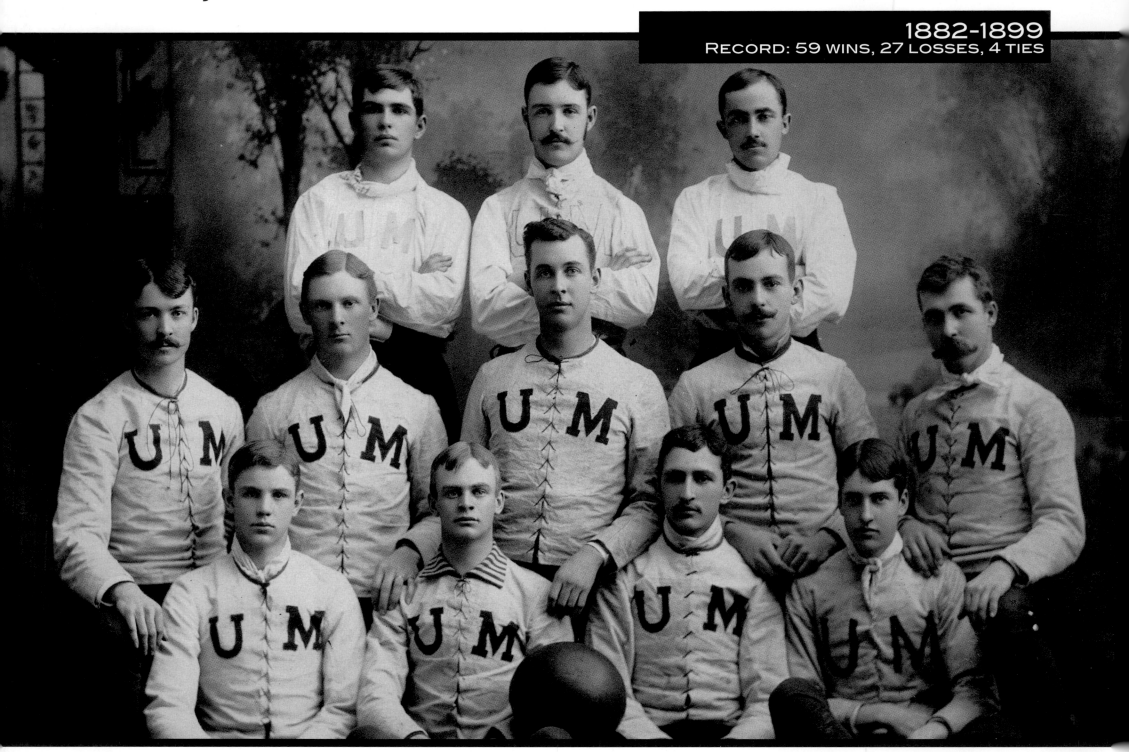

"It is pleasanter to record victories than defeats; therefore be it recorded that the University team … on the 3rd of November marched to Hamline and rattled the Wesleyans all over their own grounds."

— An account in the student newspaper *Ariel* at the end of the 1883 season.

efore there were storied players nicknamed Germany and Biggie and Bronko and Pug, and long before the unprecedented streak of national titles, there were humble beginnings to the grand game of football at the University of Minnesota.

The sport had its genesis in another era. It was different era of football, to be sure, featuring a game that bore little resemblance to today's contests. And it was another era of life in general at the state's flagship educational institution.

Six score and six years ago in 1882, the University of Minnesota was late in the tenure of its first president, William Watts Folwell, a fixture around campus known to generations of students as "Uncle Billy."

Enrollment that autumn was 222 students, and a mere handful of buildings speckled the campus landscape. It was just nine years earlier that the school had its first two graduates — chaps by the names of Warren Clark Eustis and Henry Martyn Williamson. The good folks of Minneapolis feted them with a public banquet.

Bucolic though the campus was, some fireworks had flared that spring. A group of young rapscallions, displeased at receiving too many demerits, were rumored to be heading to Folwell's house for a demonstration. Professors William A. Pike and Ira Moore headed there, too, to lend their moral support for the president. At the urging of his wife, Pike packed a pistol. As the events of the evening played out, he managed to shoot one of the students accidentally.

The wound was minor, and Uncle Billy tended to the student until a doctor arrived. Still, the event gave a bit of unwanted publicity to the fledgling land-grant university.

All was calm again in late September of that year when the school engaged in its first intercollegiate football game.

THE NON-ARRIVING BALL

Even before a contest was arranged with an off-campus foe, the game of football had been kicking around in Minnesota for a few years.

Early organized attempts at playing football on campus originated in 1878, nine years after the Rutgers-Princeton game in 1869 — the first intercollegiate football contest on record. On Oct. 30, 1878, the Minnesota student newspaper *Ariel* reported, "Football has been the all-absorbing amusement for the past weeks."

(Preceding page) The 1887 University of Minnesota team was coached by Frederick S. Jones, a Yale man, who brought the rugby style of football to the Midwest. The '87 squad was the university's first unbeaten team — at 2-0. (Right) Alfred Pillsbury was one of the early towering figures at Minnesota. He played seven years for the Gophers and made one major contribution: He owned the only football on campus. His father, John Sargent Pillsbury, is considered "The Father of the University."

1882-1899

10 BIG GAMES REMEMBERED:
1882-1899

Sept. 30, 1882: Minnesota 4, Hamline 0, in Minneapolis. Minnesota played its first game against Hamline University in a challenge at the fairgrounds. The first points were scored by A.J. Baldwin. The ending was notable. At 5:30 p.m. the Hamline players announced that they needed to leave because they promised to be back at "half-past six," and if they were late, the faculty wouldn't allow them to come play again.

In 1889, the team was coached by committee. Four men — D.W. and Al McCord, Frank Heffelfinger and Billy Morse — are listed as coaches. It worked, because the Gophers went 3-1, and all three victories were by shutout.

10 BIG GAMES REMEMBERED:
1882-1899

Nov. 12, 1883: Carleton 4, Minnesota 2, in Northfield. Minnesota had secured the services of its first coach, Thomas Peebles, who had arrived in the fall from Princeton. Peebles took his team 40 miles south to take on Carleton, which was insistent on playing a faculty member named Selden Bacon. The Gophers agreed to the request, but only if Peebles would be allowed to officiate the game. Despite having a friendly referee, Minnesota lost its first road test.

Games were typically challenges among classes, one of the first being a contest of freshmen versus sophomores, with the freshmen winning due to a decided advantage in numbers. According to an announcement in the student paper, one early interclass contest had to be cancelled "owing to the non-arrival of the ball."

The first recorded game against another college occurred Sept. 30, 1882, at the fairgrounds in Minneapolis. Three schools — the University of Minnesota, Hamline University and Carleton College — had arranged to meet that day to plan for an athletic league of the trio. Various track events were on the docket, and a football game was supposed to conclude the day's activities.

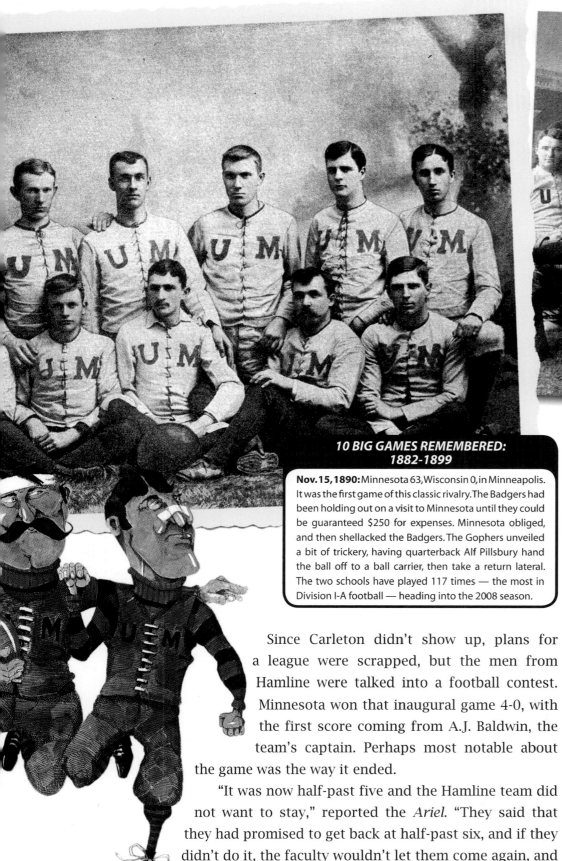

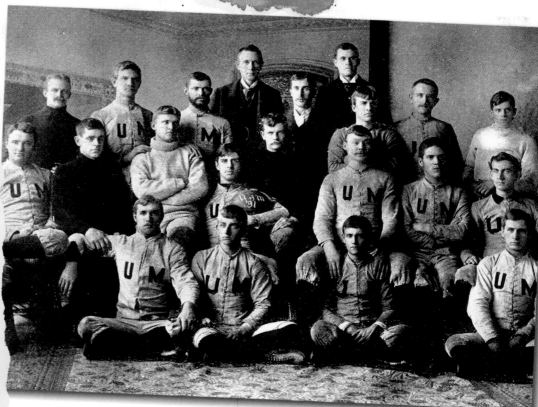

(Left) The 1890 team was the first squad to play an out-of-state school when it faced Wisconsin. The Gophers and Badgers have played 117 times since then, making it the longest rivalry in collegiate football.
(Above) In 1891, Minnesota made its first venture outside state borders, playing at Grinnell and Iowa in the span of three days. The Gophers tied Grinnell and beat Iowa, the first meeting against that long-standing rival.

10 BIG GAMES REMEMBERED: 1882-1899

Nov. 15, 1890: Minnesota 63, Wisconsin 0, in Minneapolis. It was the first game of this classic rivalry. The Badgers had been holding out on a visit to Minnesota until they could be guaranteed $250 for expenses. Minnesota obliged, and then shellacked the Badgers. The Gophers unveiled a bit of trickery, having quarterback Alf Pillsbury hand the ball off to a ball carrier, then take a return lateral. The two schools have played 117 times — the most in Division I-A football — heading into the 2008 season.

Since Carleton didn't show up, plans for a league were scrapped, but the men from Hamline were talked into a football contest. Minnesota won that inaugural game 4-0, with the first score coming from A.J. Baldwin, the team's captain. Perhaps most notable about the game was the way it ended.

"It was now half-past five and the Hamline team did not want to stay," reported the *Ariel*. "They said that they had promised to get back at half-past six, and if they didn't do it, the faculty wouldn't let them come again, and besides they didn't really like the idea of playing on a race track. It is only fair to say that the Hamlines did not have their full strength and the University won by two goals in 55 minutes. This ended the day and the crowd dispersed well satisfied with the beginning which had been made in intercollegiate sports."

Hamline, it turns out, was not entirely satisfied with that beginning, and a couple weeks later got its revenge, beating Minnesota 2-0 in a rematch. It should be noted that touchdowns only counted two points that season.

In 1883, professor Thomas Peebles was brought in from Princeton to teach mental and moral philosophy at Minnesota. Apparently, word got out to some players that Peebles was acquainted with football from his time at Princeton. He was tapped to share some tips and help the men prepare for an upcoming game with Carleton a few miles to the south in Northfield, which just seven years earlier had been the site of the famed Great Northfield Bank Robbery staged by the infamous James-Younger Gang.

Despite having its first coach, Minnesota dropped the game 4-2 to Carleton. In their other two games that fall, the Gophers defeated Hamline and a team from Minneapolis.

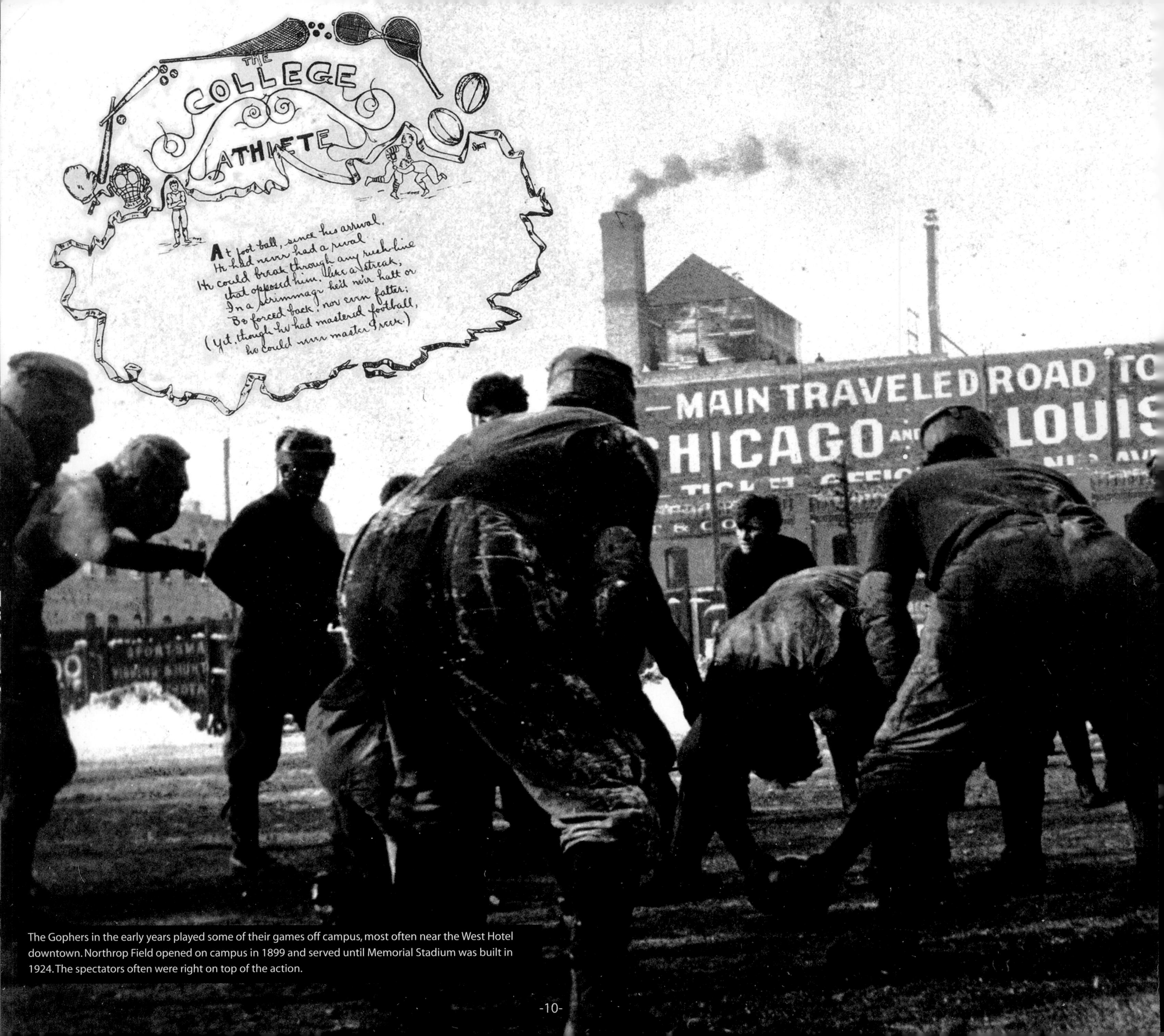

MAIN TRAVELED ROAD TO
CHICAGO AND LOUIS
THE COLLEGE ATHLETE
At foot ball, since his arrival,
He had never had a rival
He could break through any rush-line
that opposed him, like a streak;
In a scrimmage he'd ne'er halt or
Be forced back, nor even falter;
(Yet, though he had mastered football,
he could never master Greek.)

The Gophers in the early years played some of their games off campus, most often near the West Hotel downtown. Northrop Field opened on campus in 1899 and served until Memorial Stadium was built in 1924. The spectators often were right on top of the action.

Ariel summed up the season as follows:

"The University football team has been having a round of picnics, until they ventured away off to Northfield, where they received a severe drubbing at the hands, or feet, rather, of the Northfield Carleton Farmer's Alliance Football Association. It is pleasanter to record victories than defeats; therefore be it recorded that the University team beat the Minneapolis Football Association ignominiously on the 29th of October … [and] that on the 3rd of November they marched to Hamline and rattled the Wesleyans all over their own grounds, beating them by a score of 5 games to none."

In 1884 and 1885, there were no games played with outside teams, though intramural games were still played on campus.

"The Father Of The University"

As instrumental as Peebles was in getting football off the ground at the University of Minnesota, a man hired two years later was even more significant. Frederick S. Jones arrived in 1885, the first of a series of men from Yale who brought their Eastern football sensibilities to Minnesota. While Peebles preferred a soccer style of football — which may have turned off potential opponents — Jones favored the rugby style of play, which had taken favor back East.

The latter was destined to win out, in this case helped by the arrival — rather than the "non-arrival" — of a rugby ball owned by one Alfred "Alf" Pillsbury. It may not have been the only ball in town, but it was the only ball on campus.

The name Pillsbury is well known in Minnesota — flour, football and statesmanship are all ingredients of its renown. John Sargent Pillsbury, Alf's father, is to this day considered "The Father of the University." A one-time hardware merchant to whom the university owed money, Pillsbury became a regent and went to great lengths to get the school completely out from under its debt. He also served five terms as a state senator and three terms as Minnesota's governor.

At the dedication of Pillsbury's statue on campus Sept. 12, 1900, the president of the Alumni Association said, "The very existence of this university itself is due to him more than any other man." Few would dispute that claim.

If the elder Pillsbury was "The Father of the University," you could certainly count Alf as one of its favorite sons. Pillsbury, or "Pilly" as he was also known, played for the Gophers for seven seasons from 1886 to 1893, captaining the 1887 and 1889 teams. There were no term limits for football participation in those days.

Jones had come to the university after a brief teaching and coaching stint

The Gophers didn't have a coach in 1892, and apparently they didn't need one. They went 5-0 and won the Intercollegiate Athletic Association of the Northwest, thus becoming the self-proclaimed "Champions of the Northwest." Michigan, Wisconsin and Northwestern were the other members of the league, which lasted only two years.

at Shattuck Military Academy, a prep school in Faribault, Minnesota, and he coached the Gophers for three years. Given his previous connection, it was no surprise when Shattuck appeared regularly on Minnesota's schedule.

In 1886, the Gophers played Shattuck twice. The first meeting was in Faribault, and on the way down, the team developed a set of signals to use in the game, which apparently were to little avail, as it lost 9-5. A rematch at home was no more successful, with Minnesota falling 18-8 in the first game to which admission was charged.

PUDGE SIGNS UP

Two years later, Shattuck was again on the schedule twice, and after a 16-8 loss on the road — at which a contingent of Gophers rooters came along for the first time — Minnesota was finally able to prevail against the pesky prepsters 14-0 at home.

In 1887, Pillsbury was counting his troops before a game and noticed he was one Gopher short of a whole. A student from Minneapolis Central High School who was there to watch the game — a strapping 200-pound specimen — was asked by Pilly to play in the game. That lad was William Walter "Pudge" Heffelfinger, who played for Minnesota for the rest of the season before venturing eastward to Yale in 1888.

At Yale, Pudge was a three-time All-America guard and was later elected to the College Football Hall of Fame. He would also become the nation's first professional football player — getting paid $500 to play for a team in Pittsburgh — and was elected to the Pro Football Hall of Fame.

In an article in the late 1930s, Pillsbury recalled his many years playing at Minnesota and how his team was in top shape, often running five miles around the field in the morning in addition to practicing in the afternoon.

"Condition? We were really in condition," he recalled. "I remember an afternoon when we played a long, hard game on the field in the back of the West Hotel in Minneapolis and then ran the three or four miles back to the campus after the game. I wonder if the boys could do that today?"

Given that "the boys" are still playing their games in downtown Minneapolis at the Hubert H. Humphrey Metrodome, it at least remains a possibility.

The field adjacent to the West Hotel was one of the game venues for the Gophers, who were without a suitable home on campus until Northrop Field was built in 1899.

In 1890, Minnesota's football program went "scientific." The team's management procured a professional trainer named Tom Eck, who doubled as the coach, and utilized a "training table" or team meal where diets could be monitored, and strategy and signals rehearsed.

It also secured quarters in the basement of the YMCA building, a humble space that contained exactly one bathtub for the entire team. To add insult to injury, cold water was the only option on tap.

That building, constructed in 1888, still stands in the Historic Knoll District, a silent reminder of the fledgling early years. One of the five original buildings on the Twin Cities campus, it was recently put up for lease to the general public.

It turns out the scientific method was a formula for success. After mauling Hamline and Shattuck on the road to open the 1890 season, the Gophers downed Grinnell 18-13 in a snowstorm.

An Historical Drubbing

That set the stage for a bit of history — Minnesota's first game with the University of Wisconsin. The neighbors to the east had been holding out on a visit to Minnesota without a guarantee of $250 to pay for expenses, and their badgering finally worked.

Other than the payout, Minnesota was a less-than-gracious host, pummeling Wisconsin 63-0 in something of an upset. Pillsbury and company used a bit of trickery in the game to dodge the rule that required the quarterback, Pillsbury, to hand the ball off instead of advancing it himself. Minnesota's ploy that day was for Pillsbury to take a return lateral from the ball carrier, and he reeled off a number of large gains.

"The game was one continual procession towards the Wisconsin goal," recounted the *Minnesota Alumni Weekly*, "and only once, for a few seconds, did Wisconsin come within spy-glass distance of Minnesota's goal line."

REPRODUCTION

10 BIG GAMES REMEMBERED: 1882-1899

Nov. 11, 1893: Minnesota 40, Wisconsin 0, in Minneapolis. Wisconsin's captain, T.U. Lyman, had previously played against the Gophers as a member of the Grinnell team and had a distaste for Minnesota. As the story goes, he vowed that he would not leave college until he played on a squad that beat the Gophers. He would have to wait a bit longer, as the home team took it to the Badgers in dominating fashion.

1. Larson. 3. Pillsbury. 5. Danner. 7. Spicer. 9. Southworth.
2. Behlen. 4. Finlayson. 6. Cutler. 8. Stout. 10. Adams.

1. Walker. 3. Dalrymple. 5. Muir. 7. Larson, A. 9. Bisbee.
2. Harding. 4. Leary. 6. Madigan. 8. Van Campen.

(Above) Moses Taylor, Augustus Larson and his brother, whose first name has been lost to history, led the Gophers in 1894. Augustus Larson was the team captain in 1895. (Left) Composite photos of the unbeaten 1893 team, the last of Pillsbury's seven seasons as a player. From 1891-94, Minnesota had an 18-game unbeaten streak.

1882-1899

With the exception of 1906, when President Theodore Roosevelt put a freeze on heated rivalries because of a number of deaths and serious on-field injuries, Minnesota and Wisconsin have met every year since 1890. The series now stands at 117 games, making it the most-played rivalry in Division I-A football history.

The following year, under the guidance of Ed "Dad" Moulton, Minnesota played its first games out of state. A 12-12 tie against Grinnell was followed two days later by a 42-4 victory against Iowa in Iowa City, making for a successful journey.

In 1892 a new league — the Intercollegiate Athletic Association of the Northwest — was formed with Minnesota, Michigan, Northwestern and Wisconsin. Minnesota set about to lay claim at having the best 11 players in the league.

Mission accomplished. The Gophers rolled past all five opponents, including their three new association brethren, en route to their second undefeated season — the 1887 team had gone 2-0 — and the title "Champions of the Northwest."

(Left) George Finlayson, center, and the Harding brothers played for Walt "Pudge" Heffelfinger in 1895, which was the Pro Football and College Football Hall of Famer's only season as the Gophers' coach. (Below) Johnny Campbell didn't play, but he made history just the same when he organized college football's first group of cheerleaders in 1898.

10 BIG GAMES REMEMBERED:
1882-1899

Nov. 12, 1898: Minnesota 17, Northwestern 6, in Minneapolis. Cheerleading was born in college football. The Gophers' season had been in a tailspin — there had been a stretch of three straight losses — and the student body was looking for a boost. It came via an unlikely source, a student named Johnny Campbell who brought a group of "yell leaders" to the game. The Gophers responded with their only conference win of the season.

10 BIG GAMES REMEMBERED:
1882-1899

Oct. 25, 1895: Minnesota 10, Chicago 6, in Chicago. In Walt "Pudge" Heffelfinger's lone year as head coach, the Gophers traveled to Chicago and Lafayette, Indiana, for two games in four days. The first of those was a hard-fought, come-from-behind victory. The Gophers trailed 6-4 but mounted a comeback in the final five minutes and got the winning touchdown on a plunge. Minnesota was driving again when

Notable that year was a 14-6 win against Michigan, the first meeting ever between two schools that would go on to have a long and storied rivalry, later spiced with a traveling trophy bearing an even more colorful tale.

With coach "Wallie" Winter at the helm, 1893 produced a second straight undefeated campaign, six wins and no losses, including a fourth consecutive win over Wisconsin, 40-0. Unfortunately, there was no formal recognition for the efforts, because due to financial woes, the athletic association had disbanded.

The latter years of the century were characterized by a lack of continuity. Coaches — who acted more as "elder statesmen of strategy," according to university historian James Gray — came and went, rarely lasting more than a year.

Winter was followed by Thomas Cochrane Jr. in 1894, the legendary Walt "Pudge" Heffelfinger in 1895 and Alexander Jerrems in 1896 and 1897 — and they were all Yale men. Jerrems was succeeded by Jack Minds, a former All-American fullback from Pennsylvania, and then a tandem of Minnesota alums — John Harrison and William C. Leary — in 1899.

Heffelfinger's squad was enigmatic. There were two hard-fought victories — a come-from-behind 10-6 win at Chicago and a 14-10 affair versus Wisconsin. But losses to Grinnell, Purdue and Michigan in Detroit left the season less than an unmitigated success.

(Below) The team gets in some practice in 1896. The players routinely suffered broken bones, and some had an ear bloodied, like the third player from the left. (Above right) Alexander Jerrems was the coach in the first year of the Western Conference, which later evolved into the Big Ten Conference. Jerrems went 12-6 in two seasons.

10 BIG GAMES REMEMBERED: 1882-1899

Nov. 24, 1898: Illinois 11, Minnesota 10, in Minneapolis. The season finale of 1898 was played on Thanksgiving Day at the athletic field next to the West Hotel downtown. Conditions were brutal, as the temperature hovered near 10-below zero after a snowstorm had dumped several feet of snow. The field had been cleared, and snow was piled on the sidelines higher than the players' heads. At one point the ball became lost in a snowbank for a few minutes.

(Above) The 1897 Gophers in action on the field next to the West Hotel. The club went 4-4 but was winless in the Western Conference and finished last. (Opposite page) The 1898 team fared a bit better in the conference, winning once. It was also the last team to play on the fields off campus. Northrop Field came into play the next season.

Gimme An "M"

Nonetheless, Heffelfinger left an impression on his players, if not for his coaching, then for his inarguable athletic prowess.

George A.E. Finlayson, a lineman for the Gophers from 1893 to 1897, once recounted how Pudge would demonstrate to the team how to block for a halfback, instructing the varsity defense on the field to try to get at the ball carrier. "The opposing players would be sprawled on the ground all the way to the goal line in the wake of Pudge," said Finlayson.

In 1896, seven teams banded together to form the Western Conference, the precursor to the Big Ten. Minnesota joined Chicago, Illinois, Michigan, Northwestern, Purdue and Wisconsin in the league. Four years later, Indiana and Iowa joined the conference to make it the "Big Nine." Ohio State came aboard in 1912. Michigan, which left the conference in 1906, rejoined in 1917 to round out the Big Ten.

From 1896 until the end of the century, the Gophers won their share of games, but their feast in non-conference contests was overshadowed by their abysmal performance in league action, where they were only 2-10 and never finished above fifth place.

But the spirits of the Gopher faithful received an unexpected pick-me-up. It was during this period that the time-honored tradition of cheerleading was born — in the Land of 10,000 Lakes.

In 1898, the Gophers had suffered through a stretch of three straight losses, and an editorial in the school paper made a plea for help: "Any plan that would stir up enthusiasm for athletics would be helpful."

Student Johnny Campbell stepped up and offered to lead cheers at games, and it seemed as if his "yell leaders" pepped up the team during a 17-6 victory over Northwestern. The rest is ongoing history.

Many of the captains in those years doubled as the team's stars: Baldwin, who scored the first-ever points in 1882, John W. Adams, Howard T. Abbott, Pillsbury, B.E. Trask, Horace R. Robinson, William C. Leary, James E. Madigan, Everhart P. Harding, Augustus T. Larson, John M. Harrison and Henry A. "Buzz" Scandrett — with the middle initials somehow an appropriate stamp of 19th-century formality. Harrison was the first Gopher player to be named all-conference, a distinction he earned in 1896 and 1897. With the passing of the decades, even centuries, few remain as household names, with the exception of "Pillsbury," a name still in many a household's pantry.

But their footprints are an indelible mark on a bygone era.

Pilly brought the ball, Pudge brought the mystique, and Campbell brought his yells. And never underestimate that latter contribution, for there would be a lot to cheer about in the coming years.

NEXT: "Giants of the North." A doctor in the house. Slowing down "Hurry Up." "Jost left his yug." Its own breed of beast. Homegrown heroes.

1882-1899

The Giants Of The North

"What Napoleon was to France; what Alexander was to Greece; what Caesar was to Rome; what Charley Chaplin is to the flicker field … that's what Dr. Henry L. Williams is to Minnesota."

—Joe McDermott of the *Minneapolis Journal* in praise of coach Henry "Doc" Williams

As dawn broke on the 20th century, Minnesota could claim considerable success on the football field to date. The cumulative record of its coaches was 58-26-4, there had been three undefeated seasons and only once since 1886 — in 1898 — had the team suffered a losing season.

But even greater success — and its attendant recognition — lay just around the corner, waiting to be tapped by a committed long-term coach. That man was Henry L. "Doc" Williams.

Williams was a Yale guy, and a scholar and athlete of considerable repute. He edited the *Yale Daily News*, and was a four-year letterwinner and left halfback on the football team, where he played with Walt "Pudge" Heffelfinger and Amos Alonzo Stagg.

His greatest fame, though, was in track. As a senior, he set the world record in the 120-yard high hurdles, becoming the first person to run it under 16 seconds at 15.8. He also set a collegiate record in the low hurdles at 25.2 seconds. Later, Williams was an honors student in medicine at the University of Pennsylvania.

He became the first salaried coach at Minnesota, signing a three-year contact for $2,500 a year. He also practiced medicine, which was a handy skill set in the rough-and-tumble, padding-scarce early years of football.

While grateful for the opportunity at Minnesota, Williams was less than impressed with the facilities he was inheriting. Years later he shared his thoughts on his new terrain:

"On arriving in Minneapolis in the middle of August 1900, a view of Northrop Field as it then was, was anything but prepossessing and encouraging. … Soft sandy loam, bare of turf but well sprinkled with weeds and sand burrs covered the surface of the ground. But a pair of goal posts at either end of the lot and a narrow row of seats extending along the fence furnished evidence that this was the Minnesota football field."

Williams wasn't the first person to take a poke at the burr-ridden field stretching across what is now the Historic Knoll Area of campus. But it was on this field and its replacement a few years later that the University of Minnesota, under the guidance of Henry L. Williams, would emerge as a northern powerhouse.

FROM EXASPERATION TO EXHILARATION

His team of 1900 was not big — certainly not by today's standards — but every man on Williams' first team was at least 6 feet tall, which earned the boys the nickname "The Giants of the North."

Though that name was not without appeal, Williams would bristle when his team was referred to as "Minnesota beef," especially when compared to so-called "Chicago brains."

Williams himself was long on football IQ, and he is credited with a number of innovations to the game, including crisscross plays and other razzle dazzle, the

season and a Western Conference championship.

Minnesota's success under first-year coach Williams was followed with more of the same. The 1901 team, captained by Warren Knowlton, outscored its opponents 183-18 on its way to a 9-1-1 record, with the only scars being another 0-0 tie with those pesky boys from Minneapolis Central and an 18-0 loss at unbeaten Wisconsin.

In both 1901 and 1902, Minnesota finished with a 3-1 record in the Western Conference, good for third place.

SLOWING DOWN "HURRY UP"

Then came 1903, a year that put a dent in a dynasty, christened a new juggernaut and gave birth to college football's most famous crock.

In the summer of '03 — through the cooperation of Gov. John Sargent Pillsbury and the generosity of his

WISCONSIN GAME

LUXTON MPLS. JOURNAL

revolving wedge and the "Minnesota shift" in which the interior linemen and ends adjusted right before the snap of the ball.

His coaching debut was inauspicious, to say the least, with the squad struggling to a 0-0 tie against Minneapolis Central High School, a game that the *Minnesota Daily* student newspaper deemed "exasperating."

Exasperation quickly turned to exhilaration. The Gophers shut out their next four opponents — St. Paul Central High, Macalester, Carleton and Iowa State — by a combined 163-0.

That set up a mid-October match with Chicago, which had thumped Minnesota 29-0 in the season finale a year earlier. This would be a true test of where Williams' men stood.

They stood up to the challenge and then some, outplaying Chicago considerably in a 6-6 tie. At halftime of the game, a Chicago fan with a megaphone was heard to announce, "We have met the enemy and we are theirs."

Two more shutouts followed, 26-0 against Grinnell and 34-0 over North Dakota, before Minnesota met another true test against Wisconsin. The visitors from Madison gave the Gophers all they could handle, especially in the second half. Twice the Badgers got inside the 5-yard line but failed to score — the last time falling just 6 inches short of the goal line — as Minnesota prevailed 6-5.

(Below) A Minnesota player struggles for yardage against Wisconsin in 1900. The Gophers scored only once but it was enough for a 6-5 victory over the Badgers. Outside of two ties, it was the closest game Minnesota had during Williams' first season.

10 BIG GAMES REMEMBERED:

son, Alfred — the old Northrop Field was realigned and given a facelift. Greater Northrop Field was increased to about three times its previous size, with a seating capacity of about 20,000, and surrounded with a 10-foot brick wall, courtesy of Alfred, the former Gopher player and captain.

The Gophers appeared quite comfortable in their new digs, and in their first 10 games felt no urge to extend much hospitality — much less surrender points — to their Midwestern guests.

After the requisite early-season games with high school foes, Minnesota went on another shutout frenzy, beating Carleton 29-0, Macalester 112-0, Grinnell 39-0, Hamline 65-0, Iowa State 46-0, Iowa 75-0 and Beloit 46-0.

That set up an Oct. 31 showdown with the University of Michigan, a team coached by Fielding "Hurry Up" Yost, who had been scripting his own legend over the past few seasons. As prolific as Williams' bunch had been in the early part of the decade, Yost's teams had put up even more jaw-dropping numbers. Michigan came to town riding a 29-game winning streak, and in the previous two and a half seasons had outscored its opponents 1,631-12. Its offense had averaged 56 points a game during that stretch, and at one point scored 600 points in 10 games, earning the nickname "Point-A-Minute."

(Top left) A full house is on hand for the 1902 homecoming game against Wisconsin, an 11-0 Gophers victory. (Above) A big crowd was also on hand for an early game in 1901. (Opposite page, top right) The Gophers punch across one of their touchdowns against the Badgers in the '02 homecoming game.

It would be hard to produce evidence that another game in Minnesota history was as eagerly anticipated. The local newspapers filled pages and pages with hype and conjecture, and Minnesotans responded with ravenous interest.

By midmorning, enterprising fans had begun scurrying up trees and telegraph poles with a view of the field, and the grandstand was filled to capacity well before the 2:30 p.m. kickoff.

Minnesota owned the advantage throughout the first half, racking up 17 first downs compared to two for the Wolverines. After a scoreless first half, Minnesota drove to the 8-yard line before Michigan's defense stiffened and the Wolverines finally launched a counterattack. Michigan took the lead when All-American halfback Willie Heston scored from a yard out on his ninth carry on a long drive.

With just moments remaining in the contest, Minnesota's Egil Boeckman finally found the end zone, the first points allowed by Michigan all season. James Kremer "punted out," which gave the Gophers a better angle for the conversion, and Ed Rogers kicked the point after to make the score 6-6.

DIAGRAM OF THE GAME.

FIRST HALF

5 10 15 20 25 30 35 40 45 50 55 50 45 40 35 30 25 20 15 10 5

MINN. GOAL

MICH. GOAL

SECOND HALF

October 31st 1903

MINN. GOAL

TOUCHDOWN & GOAL

MICH. GOAL

TOUCHDOWN & GOAL

TIME CALLED —

AAA = PENALTY
M = MINNESOTA BALL
M = MICHIGAN BALL
P = MINN. FUMBLE
M = MICH.
O = DOWN
- - - = MINNESOTA
— = MICHIGAN
CURVED LINES = KICKS

REPRODUCTION

The 1903 matchup with mighty Michigan was perhaps the most highly anticipated game ever in over a century of Minnesota football. The stands were full and some enterprising fans crawled up telegraph poles to watch. Fancy carriages — horseless and otherwise — were much in evidence. (Inset, opposite page) The original Little Brown Jug — "captured'" by custodian Oscar Munson — has been contested by Minnesota and Michigan ever since then.

When Minnesota had tied mighty Michigan, the crowd went wild and rushed out onto the field. The team captains called the game at that point, likely for a combination of looming darkness and the on-field pandemonium.

No matter. Yost's scoring machine had been effectively silenced and Michigan's winning streak retired.

The local papers proclaimed victory the following day. Headlines in the *Minneapolis Sunday Tribune* included: "Victory, though the score is tied," "Yost and Michigan Practically Beaten" and "Minnesota Supreme in Western Football." In this case, a tie appeared every bit as good as a win.

"Jost Left His Yug"

The game itself was only part of the legacy of that Halloween day in 1903. After the game, Minnesota custodian Oscar Munson discovered a five-gallon earthenware water jug that Michigan had left behind, and brought it to the office of Louis Cooke, head of the athletic department.

Munson, a Norwegian immigrant who had difficulty pronouncing the letters "j" and "y," announced to Cooke, "Jost left his yug." From there, they painted on it "Michigan Jug — Captured by Oscar, October 31, 1903," along with the score, "Minnesota 6, Michigan 6" with an enlarged "6" for Minnesota.

(Top right) Egil Boeckman punches across for the tying touchdown against Michigan. (Far right) Williams prowls the sidelines during the Michigan game. (Below) The "yug," as Munson called it, has even been celebrated in song. The Glenn Miller recording of it was a big hit in the 1940s.

Little Brown Jug

Words and music by
Joseph E. Winner(?)

Lively

C   F   Dm   G7   C   G   C

mf
1. My wife and I lived all a lone, in a lit-tle log hut we called our own;

Northrop Field was expanded in 1903 because of the increased demand for seats. A 10-foot fence went up around the field, courtesy of Alf Pillsbury, the former player. The Gophers celebrated their new home by going 14-0-1 and outscoring the opposition 618-12.

Yost later wrote to Cooke asking him to return the jug, and Cooke responded, "If you want it, you'll have to win it." The teams didn't play each other again until 1909, but from that point on, the winner has taken home the Little Brown Jug, which is now half maroon and half blue with the scores of all the rivalry games painted on it. The jug is hands-down the most famous traveling trophy in all of college football.

A number of Minnesota's earliest football heroes had a hand in the Michigan game.

There was captain Rogers, who kicked the tying point and was one of two Native Americans on the team. Rogers was born in northern Minnesota near Big Sandy Lake, the son of an Ojibwe mother and a Scottish-Irish father. Though not an All-America selection, Rogers was elected to the College Football Hall of Fame in 1968. He went on to practice law for 62 years in Walker, Minnesota, and served as county attorney for more than 40 of those years.

There was All-American Fred "Germany" Schacht, who, at 210 pounds, was the heaviest lineman on the Gophers. At the same time, he was fast enough to be the Gophers' leading rusher. Three years after playing for the Gophers, Schacht died of kidney disease.

Yet another of the 1903 Gophers was end Bobby Marshall, the first of Minnesota's African-American athletes and a 1971 inductee to the College Football Hall of Fame. The term "athlete" barely does Marshall justice. His football career began in 1899 at Minneapolis Central High School and didn't end until he was 54 years old. He earned letters in football, track and baseball, playing first base on the league champion Gopher team of 1907. He played pro football, semi-pro baseball and even pro hockey.

Its Own Breed Of Beast

If Minnesota was a giant slayer in its famous tie with Michigan in 1903, it became its own breed of beast in 1904, destroying everything in its path and leaving innumerable footprints in the end zone.

After drubbing the St. Paul and Minneapolis Central high schools by a combined 107-0 in a doubleheader to open the season, the Gophers proceeded to run up incredible scores against three regional foes — 77-0 against South Dakota, 75-0 against Shattuck Academy and 65-0 against Carleton.

The next three weeks saw relatively modest offensive output — 114 points in shutout wins against St. Thomas, North Dakota and Iowa State. But Minnesota poured it on the following week, beating Grinnell by the remarkable score of 146-0, with 73 points scored in each half. Grinnell failed to make a first down, and the Gophers rarely needed a second attempt

10 BIG GAMES REMEMBERED: 1900-1921

Oct. 22, 1904: Minnesota 146, Grinnell 0, in Minneapolis. The Gophers outscored Grinnell 73-0 — in the first half alone — then proceeded to do the same thing in the second half en route to a 146-0 victory over their regional rival, setting the record for scoring in a game. Minnesota moved up and down the field virtually at will while holding Grinnell to no first downs for the entire game. The previous scoring mark had been held by Michigan in a 130-0 win over West Virginia.

(Above) An artist's rendition of a 1904 game shows the packed house at "new" Northrop Field.

FREDERIC

1900-1921

SUNDAY PIONEER PRESS, NOV. 15, 1953 SECOND NEWS SECTION c FIFTEEN

DO YOU REMEMBER?

BLACK DERBIES BY THE DOZEN topped the heads of these sportswriters covering a football game at the University of Minnesota's old Northrop field about 1904. In this pre-Paul Giel scene, two newsmen behind the table have been identified. They are (far left) J. Alec Sloan, St. Paul Daily News sports writer, and (third from left) Joseph E. Hennessy, St. Paul Globe political writer and father of Joe Hennessy, current Pioneer Press sports editor.

10 BIG GAMES REMEMBERED: 1900-1921

Nov. 12, 1904: Minnesota 28, Wisconsin 0, in Minneapolis. The Gophers notched their 10th shutout win of the season 28-0 against Wisconsin in front of 18,000 fans at Greater Northrop Field. Heading into the game, Minnesota had outscored its opponents 668-12, averaging 1.5 points a minute. The Gophers outgained the Badgers from scrimmage 641 yards to 52. James Kremer scored three touchdowns for Minnesota and O.N. Davies added two more scores.

Gentlemen of the press take in the action. A reporter of the era would file a running account of the game via Morse code by using the telegraph key in front of him. (Opposite page) How a player circa 1904 looked. The next year, the sport was almost banned by President Theodore Roosevelt because of the violence, but rules changes in 1906 averted such drastic action.

to gain one. The maroon and gold broke the record for most points in a game, held previously by Michigan in a 130-0 victory over West Virginia and later eclipsed by Georgia Tech against Cumberland 222-0.

Nebraska would score the only points against Minnesota that season the following week, but the Gophers still prevailed 16-12. Four more shutout wins would follow, including 69-0 against Lawrence and 28-0 against Wisconsin, games in which the Gophers racked up nearly 1,200 yards of offense.

That team, led by All-American end Moses Strathern, finished the season with a mark of 13-0 and a share of the conference title. Even more amazing were the point totals and differentials for the season. Minnesota outscored the opposition by a total of 725-12, or an average of 55-1 per game.

Ten more wins and a similar number of gaudy scores were to follow in 1905, with the only blemish being a 16-12 loss to Wisconsin, which cost the Gophers a share of another league title.

In 1906, the famed Carlisle Indian Industrial School appeared on the Gophers' schedule. This was in the Indians' heyday, and they came to Minnesota to hand the home team its only defeat of the season 17-0.

THE "PURITY BANQUET"

Also that year, Minnesota renewed a rivalry with the University of Chicago — which had been interrupted since the 6-6 tie of 1900 — and a tradition featuring a "purity banquet" that Williams would write about a decade later. This involved the home team hosting a social dinner the evening before the battle, ostensibly leading to good sportsmanship and a clean game.

Lest anyone think Williams was prepossessed to crave the purity banquet and all of its wholesomeness, his assessment of it was a bit restrained: "While well-intended and carried out according to agreement, Minnesota has nevertheless found this dinner with its attendant speech-making often drawn out, somewhat tiring in connection with the nervous strain present on the night preceding a crucial contest."

The legendary Jim Thorpe led Carlisle to another victory over Minnesota in 1907, but this time by a slim margin of 12-10. With a 2-2-1 mark — including 0-1-1 in the conference — this was the first team of Williams' to finish without a winning record.

The Gophers finished 3-2-1 but failed to win a conference game in 1908. However, they were able to pull off an 11-6 upset over Carlisle in the season finale when they employed the forward pass extensively for the first time.

The target of many of those

10 BIG GAMES REMEMBERED: 1900-1921

Nov. 21, 1908: Minnesota 11, Carlisle 6, in Minneapolis. Minnesota used the forward pass with great success in scoring an upset victory over an eastern powerhouse — the Carlisle Indians, featuring legendary Jim Thorpe. The Gophers scored on touchdown runs by A.F. Plankers and Lyle Johnston, while Carlisle notched its only score on a touchdown by Afraid-of-a-Bear. The Gophers surprised the Indians with their passing attack by completing 10 of 15 attempts.

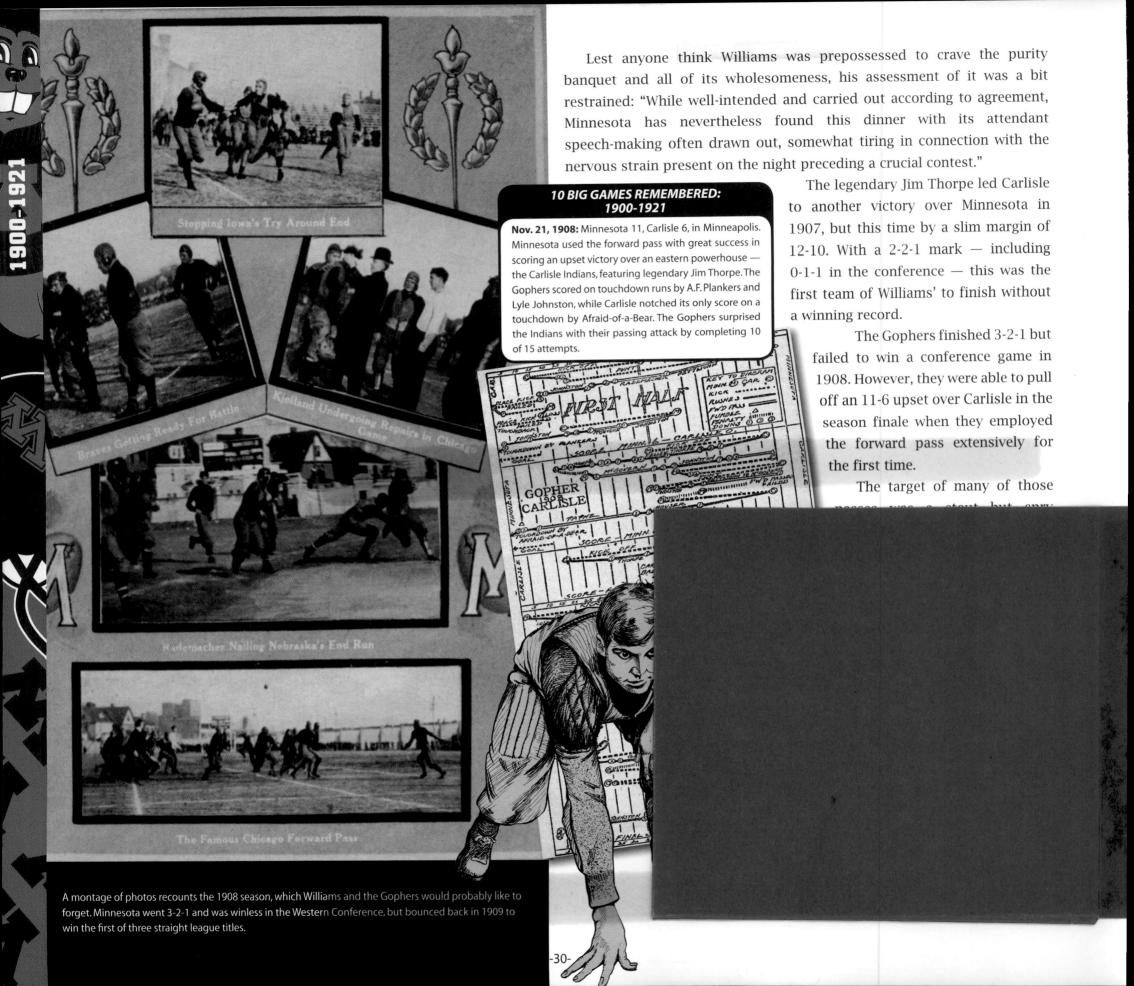

Stopping Iowa's Try Around End

Braves Getting Ready For Battle

Kjelland Undergoing Repairs in Chicago Game

Rademacher Nailing Nebraska's End Run

The Famous Chicago Forward Pass

A montage of photos recounts the 1908 season, which Williams and the Gophers would probably like to forget. Minnesota went 3-2-1 and was winless in the Western Conference, but bounced back in 1909 to win the first of three straight league titles.

-30-

(Above) Little Johnny McGovern goes for a gain in the 20-6 win over Chicago in 1909. McGovern played far bigger than his size — 5-foot-5 and 145 pounds. He is one of 20 Gophers players and coaches in the College Football Hall of Fame. He was inducted in 1966.

10 BIG GAMES REMEMBERED: 1900-1921

Oct. 30, 1909: Minnesota 20, Chicago 6, in Minneapolis. Minnesota upset Amos Alonzo Stagg's University of Chicago team at Northrop Field, setting the stage for a Western Conference championship. Johnny McGovern led the way with three drop-kick field goals before he was forced to exit the game with a broken collarbone, and the Gophers were able to tack on two additional scores to just one for Chicago. Minnesota finished 3-0 in conference play.

McGovern led the Gophers to a conference championship in 1909 and a share of the title in 1910. His three drop-kick field goals were key in a 20-6 upset of Stagg's Chicago squad in 1909.

Minnesota tacked on another co-championship in 1911 with a 6-0-1 record. In fact, the only losses from 1909 through 1911 were in two tight games with Michigan, which had left the conference over various disagreements with the league rules.

The 1913 Gophers tied for second in the league, thanks to fullback Clark Shaughnessy of St. Paul. Shaughnessy would go on to become a successful coach — with stops at Tulane, Chicago and Stanford in the college ranks and later with the NFL's Los Angeles Rams — and is known as the father of the T-formation.

CHAMPIONS OF WESTERN CONFERENCE

UNIVERSITY OF MINNESOTA FOOT BALL TEAM, '09

REPRODUCTION

10 BIG GAMES REMEMBERED: 1900-1921

Nov. 13, 1909: Minnesota 34, Wisconsin 6, in Madison. The Gophers scored a decisive win over Wisconsin at Camp Randall to win their first of three consecutive conference championships. They took the opening kickoff and marched 85 yards for a score, capped by a Lewis Stevens run. Wisconsin answered with a short score following a fumbled onside kick attempt, but then Minnesota scored 28 straight points to close out the game.

(Above) A montage of photos from the 1910 victory over Wisconsin. In their three-year run of conference titles from 1909-11, the Gophers allowed the Badgers only 12 points.

10 BIG GAMES REMEMBERED: 1900-1921

Nov. 4, 1911: Minnesota 30, Chicago 0, in Minneapolis. The Gophers downed Chicago in what some witnesses say was one of the greatest games ever played by a Minnesota team. Chicago mustered only two first downs and Minnesota's line, said one account, "was invulnerable, a veritable stone wall, against which Chicago would dash and make no impression." The Gophers scored in all manner of ways — two drop kicks, one place kick and four touchdowns.

(Top) Three Chicago defenders gang up on the Gophers' R.M. Rosenwald. (Bottom) The Maroons' defense couldn't stop Ralph Capron on his dash around end in the 1910 Minnesota-Chicago game, as the Gophers won 24-0 in the Windy City. Minnesota allowed only six points all year.

National Football Foundation and College Hall of Fame

Bert Baston

University of Minnesota 1914-1916

End 1914-16

has been granted the highest honors of The National Football Foundation and College Hall of Fame, in recognition of his outstanding playing ability as demonstrated in intercollegiate competition, his sportsmanship, integrity, character, and contribution to the sport of football, this certificate bears witness that his name shall be forever honored in the College Football Hall of Fame

Elected 1954

HOMEGROWN HEROES

Minnesota's next run at the title would come in 1915. The Gophers were led that year by a trio of homegrown All-Americans — guard Merton Dunnigan from St. Paul, end Bert Baston from St. Louis Park and halfback and captain Bernie Bierman from Litchfield.

Bierman actually took over as captain in the middle of the season for Lorin Solon, a two-time All-America end who was disqualified from amateur athletics when it was discovered he had played professional baseball in Montana under an assumed name.

After opening the season with four straight wins, the Gophers could only muster a 6-6 tie with Illinois. But they rebounded with a pair of wins for a share of the conference title, capped by a 20-3 victory over Wisconsin behind Bierman's two touchdowns and four interceptions. It was the eighth title in the Williams era, but it would be the last.

As good as Williams' teams had been in the early part of the century, as indisputable his collection of wins and titles, no team was as heralded as the 1916 squad. The Gophers were led by their first great passing combination — quarterback Arnold "Pudge" Wyman to the sure-handed two-time All-American end Baston, who would also end up in the College Hall of Fame.

Minnesota blasted its first four opponents — South Dakota State, North Dakota, South Dakota and Iowa — by a combined 236-14, and was favored by as many as 40 points against Illinois, which had already lost to Ohio State and Colgate.

So good were the Gophers that no less an authority than Walter Camp, whose name was revered in college football circles, called them "the perfect team of history." He even made the trip to Minnesota to have a look at the many players he might be naming to his All-America team.

(Right) End Bert Baston was another College Hall of Famer from the Williams era. He also served many years as an assistant coach. (Above) The certificate Baston received when he was inducted in 1954. (Inset) A Minnesota player as depicted on a 1915 program.

Band members line the sideline getting ready for the halftime show during the 1914 Wisconsin game. A capacity crowd of 17,000 watched their Gophers whip the archrival Badgers 14-3. It was the second of four straight Minnesota wins in the long series.

10 BIG GAMES REMEMBERED: 1900-1921

Nov. 20, 1915: Minnesota 20, Wisconsin 3, in Madison. Behind the stellar performance of captain Bernie Bierman, playing in his last game as a Gopher, Minnesota captured a share of the conference title. The All-American Bierman scored two touchdowns and intercepted four Wisconsin passes. A.D. Wyman tacked on the final Minnesota touchdown, and the Gophers also got fine play from C.I. "Shorty" Long and another All-American, Bert Baston.

"DOC" IN ACTION

(Above) Williams oversees his charges during a practice in 1915. The practice made almost perfect, obviously, as Minnesota went 6-0-1 and shared the Big Ten title. It was Williams' last championship. (Inset, right) Bernie Bierman was an All-American halfback. Later as the head coach of the Gophers, he led them during their most glorious era.

10 BIG GAMES REMEMBERED: 1900-1921

Nov. 4, 1916: Illinois 14, Minnesota 9, in Minneapolis. Minnesota came into this game with a 4-0 record, trouncing its opponents by a combined score of 236-14. So powerful were the Gophers that Walter Camp had called them "the perfect team of history." But Illinois surprised everyone this day by shutting down the Gophers early and taking a 14-0 lead. Minnesota came back on a touchdown run by Joe Sprafka and a late safety, but it wouldn't be enough.

But fate, along with some clever coaching and an inspired effort by Illinois, dealt a crippling blow to Minnesota's pursuit of perfection. Illinois coach Bob Zuppke had noticed a Minnesota trend of opening games with runs by three different backs in a set order — first Joe Sprafka, then Wyman, then C.I. "Shorty" Long. He told his defense to key on those three on the first series, and sure enough, that is how Williams' offense came out of the chute.

The Gophers were forced to punt and found themselves down 14-0 when Wyman threw an interception that was returned 55 yards for a touchdown. Minnesota finally answered in the second half on a 5-yard touchdown run by Sprafka and a late safety, but fell short 14-9. Perfection had met its match, at least for a day.

The Gophers rebounded admirably, taking out their frustrations with vengeance by beating Wisconsin 54-0 and dealing Stagg his worst defeat ever at Chicago 49-0. Still, the 6-1 season and third-place finish were bitter pills to swallow.

Led by All-American tackle George Hauser, the Gophers went 4-1 in 1917, the lone blemish being a 10-7 loss to Wisconsin.

Led by speedy halfback Arnie Oss in 1919, the Gophers went 4-2-1 and beat Michigan — which had returned to the conference, now called the Big Ten — in the season finale 34-7 to reclaim the Little Brown Jug, which the Wolverines had held for 10 years.

A TURN FOR THE WORSE

As Williams began his third decade at the helm of the Gophers, his fortunes took a decided turn for the worse. After opening the 1920 season with a 41-3 win over North Dakota, Minnesota lost its final six games, never scoring more than seven points along the way. The following season brought another losing record and unrest among the school's faithful.

Williams had been relying even more heavily on strategy shrouded in secrecy. When the conference mandated that all players have numbers on their jerseys, he responded with some new trickery. The players appeared for a game against Northwestern adorned with four-digit numbers, which were difficult for the university powers that be — let alone fans and scouts — to digest.

Discussions swirled about whether it was time for Williams to resign, but new President Lotus Coffman wasn't convinced. Ultimately, the debate was resolved when it was decided to restructure the governance of athletics. A new committee terminated contracts with all of Minnesota's coaches, and responsibilities were turned over to a new department overseeing both physical education and athletics.

As it turned out, all coaches who were fired were rehired with the notable exception of Williams. "Doc" retrained his focus on medicine but continued to watch his beloved Gophers from a distance — bruised but apparently not bitter.

Henry "Doc" Williams would die just nine years later in 1931, but his name lives on in a legendary athletic venue on campus. The field

house was remodeled in 1949 and renamed Williams Arena. It now carries an equally affectionate nickname, "The Barn."

In the 1919 homecoming game program, Joe McDermott, sports editor of the *Minneapolis Journal*, had this praise for the beloved doctor:

"What Napoleon was to France; what Alexander was to Greece; what Caesar was to Rome; what Charley Chaplin is to the flicker field; what the Smith Brothers are to the cough drop industry; what Andy Gump is to twentieth century existence — that's what Dr. Henry L. Williams is to Minnesota."

Few could argue what Williams had meant for University of Minnesota football. He is still the school's winningest coach — by a wide margin — at 136-33-1, for a percentage of .786. The Hall of Famer suffered but two losing seasons and finished undefeated five times.

(Above) Cheerleaders have been a staple at Minnesota games longer than at any other school. The first group was formed in 1898. Female cheerleaders didn't come along until the 1920s.

1900-1921

Under Williams' leadership, Minnesota won or shared eight conference titles. Moreover, the Gophers emerged as a western and even national powerhouse, a label that would suit them well in the coming decades.

(Right) Williams is still the winningest coach in Minnesota history at 136-33-11. Credited with many innovations in the game, he was in the first class inducted into the College Football Hall of Fame. (Below) The trophy given to Williams by all of his old players upon his retirement in 1921. (Opposite page) An architect's rendering of how the campus would look in 1909. The proposed stadium, which didn't come along until 1924, is at the upper right.

NEXT: A legend from the North. The gallant Lt. Martineau. A perfect benediction. The "Owatonna Thunderbolt." The "Mightiest Mammal of the Mat." A picture-perfect coach.

CITY OF M

EAPOLIS MINNE

CASS HIT'EC

DICOTT AST 24 T

A Legend From The North

"I have said it a thousand times. Bronko Nagurski was the greatest player I ever saw, and I saw a lot of them in my lifetime."

— Illinois' Harold "Red" Grange

Without its "doctor" to look after the health of the football family, Minnesota was faced with a coaching change for the first time since the turn of the century.

Early in 1922, six days after being named the new athletic director, Fred B. Luehring announced William Spaulding would be his first football coach at the University of Minnesota. Spaulding came to the school from Kalamazoo, where he had found success in 15 years as coach at the Western State Normal School — now called Western Michigan University. Spaulding was Minnesota's 13th head coach, but the locals had gotten out of the habit of counting coaches, with Henry "Doc" Williams having been around for so long.

Spaulding opened his tenure that fall with shutout wins at home against North Dakota and against Indiana in Indianapolis, followed by a 7-7 tie at Northwestern and Minnesota's first victory against Ohio State in two tries, by a 9-0 margin.

But the honeymoon soon passed, and November wasn't nearly as kind to the Gophers. Minnesota finished with losses to Wisconsin, Iowa and Michigan, and Spaulding's first campaign ended at a modest 3-3-1.

LT. MARTINEAU ENLISTS

Minnesota was back in championship contention the following year, due in no small measure to the exploits of All-American back Earl Martineau.

Before suiting up for Minnesota, Martineau had served as a Marine Corps lieutenant in France during World War I, and he was decorated with the Croix de Guerre and Distinguished Service Cross for gallantry.

Gallant could also describe his exploits on the gridiron. Martineau was captain of a Gophers team that finished 5-1-1 in 1923, with the only *blemishes being a midseason scoreless tie* at Wisconsin and a 10-0 setback at Michigan in the season finale — a loss made all the more unlikely by the fact that the Wolverines were able to muster only 66 rushing yards.

Martineau led Minnesota to a 13-12 victory against Haskell in the second game of the season, scoring a touchdown despite playing with a cast on his hand. He is perhaps best remembered for a spectacular defensive play in the Wisconsin game. After Badgers halfback Rollie Williams had broken into the clear, Martineau was the only defender between him and the goal line. Problem was that Williams had a convoy of blockers in front of him. In a split second, Martineau sized up his only chance, leaped over the blockers, crashed into the ball carrier and preserved the scoreless tie.

The Gophers also fashioned something of an upset over a heavier Iowa team on Nov. 17. Martineau had a hand in all three touchdowns, rushing for two and throwing to fellow All-American Ray Eklund for the third in the

(Preceding page) Enterprising fans climb up telegraph poles and trees to take in a game in 1922. The demand for tickets was making Northrop Field obsolete, but a new stadium was on the horizon. (Above) William Spaulding, the successor to Henry "Doc" Williams, coached the Gophers for three seasons before bolting for UCLA. His record at Minnesota was 11-7-4.

1922-1931

20-7 victory. That game would serve as a swan song to Greater Northrop Field, whose superlatives had faded over time.

Two years earlier, new university President Lotus D. Coffman had met with a large group of alumni to discuss the need for a new stadium, as the old one had not kept up with increasing student enrollment and burgeoning local interest in college football. The General Alumni Association then came up with the ambitious plan to garner $2 million in pledges from alumni, students and faculty to build two landmark structures on campus — an auditorium able to accommodate the entire student body and a new football stadium. The fundraising campaign was a smashing success, and the stadium — which would seat 55,000 — was chosen to be the first of the projects.

So, on a blustery, snowy day in early March 1924, a few hundred fans gathered at the corner of University Avenue and Oak Street to watch Coffman break ground for the new stadium. The cornerstone was laid in the middle of June and, amazingly, Memorial Stadium — named in honor of Minnesota veterans who had died in the service of their country — was completed in time for the opening game of that season against North Dakota, a full 42 days ahead of schedule.

A MEMORABLE DAY

However, the new stadium's official dedication came in a most memorable game on Nov. 15. The opponent that day was Illinois, which came into town with a 14-game winning streak.

Interestingly, Illinois coach Bob Zuppke's squad just happened to have dedicated its own Memorial Stadium about a month earlier in rather sensational fashion. In that game, Illinois destroyed a strong Michigan team behind the almost mythical performance of Harold "Red" Grange. Grange, who would earn the nickname "The Galloping Ghost," scored on runs of 95,

---

10 BIG GAMES REMEMBERED: 1922-1931

Oct. 13, 1923: Minnesota 13, Haskell 12, in Minneapolis. Minnesota prevailed in a squeaker against the Haskell Indians at Northrop Field. Early in the second quarter, Ray Eklund leaped high to snare a Herb Swanbeck pass in traffic for the Gophers' first score. Senior captain and halfback Earl Martineau scored Minnesota's other touchdown on a brilliant 41-yard run — despite playing the game with a cast on his hand.

A Minnesota runner goes up and over Haskell defenders in 1923, the Gophers' best year under Spaulding. The Gophers were unbeaten through the first six games before losing to Michigan in the season finale.

Minnesota's defense was the order of the day in the 1923 encounter with the Badgers. The game ended in a scoreless tie when Earl Martineau made a game-saving tackle on Wisconsin's Rollie Williams.

10 BIG GAMES REMEMBERED:
1922-1931

Oct. 27, 1923: Minnesota 0, Wisconsin 0, in Madison. It was the third tie in the rivalry that began in 1890. This game is remembered by a spectacular defensive play by Earl Martineau. After the Badgers' Rollie Williams had broken into the clear, Martineau was the only defender with a chance to catch him, but he faced a convoy of interference. Marineau leaped over the blockers and smashed into Williams to prevent the touchdown and preserve the tie.

67, 56 and 44 yards in the first quarter — the only times he touched the football and allegedly without anyone touching him. Having been engaged ...nder of the ...down pass

...ered on the ...l fans and ..., obviously

...d a 70-yard ...ame, Grange ...cknameless

...s the game ...a number of ...off any big ...rs had seen ...s rattled by a bone-jarring tackle, and a few plays later left the game for good with a shoulder injury.

And Schutte? He scampered for two touchdowns in the first half to give the Gophers the lead and tacked on an insurance touchdown in the second half.

The final totals shocked the spectators, the media and the football world: Minnesota 20, Illinois 7. Rushing yards by Schutte, 282; by Illinois, 109.

Perhaps that game helped exorcise the ghost of the ghastly loss to Illinois in 1916 by Minnesota's "perfect team." It certainly was a perfect benediction for the new Memorial Stadium.

THE "OWATONNA THUNDERBOLT"

In the spring of 1925, Spaulding resigned to become the head coach and athletic director at UCLA. His three seasons at Minnesota produced a record of 11-7-4 and a string of middle-of-the-pack finishes.

Spaulding was succeeded by Dr. Clarence Spears, who played at Dartmouth and was an All-America guard in 1915. Spears became known for a very physical style of power football, brought to bear by a series of bruising fullbacks.

The first of those was Herb Joesting, an Owatonna native who earned the nickname "Owatonna Thunderbolt." Joesting played from 1925 through

10 BIG GAMES REMEMBERED:
1922-1931

Oct. 24, 1925: Notre Dame 19, Minnesota 7, in Minneapolis. This was the first time Minnesota had ever played Notre Dame in football, and Knute Rockne's crew was coming off a national championship. The game was tied 7-7 at the half, with the Gophers narrowly missing a chance to take the lead when they fumbled on the Fighting Irish 2-yard line. In the second half, Notre Dame pulled away for the victory.

said of him, "The best way to stop Bronko was to shoot him as he was leaving the locker room."

Nagurski was not about to supplant the All-American Joesting at fullback, so he began the 1927 season by playing end on both offense and defense. In a 57-10 victory over North Dakota in the opener, he displayed a level of brawn and toughness that eventually prompted Spears to move him to tackle on defense, where he would be a fixture throughout his Gopher career.

Joesting had to sit out the second game with a knee injury, a 40-0 rout over Oklahoma A&M. Then Indiana was able to gain a 14-14 tie with Minnesota, despite collecting only five first downs compared to 17 for the Gophers.

The maroon and gold downed Iowa 38-0 and Wisconsin 13-7, setting up another encounter with Notre Dame, this time in South Bend. If the odds seemed stacked in the game against Illinois and Grange three years earlier, things looked no more promising against the Fighting Irish, which had not lost at home since 1905.

After some seesaw action, Notre Dame recovered a fumbled punt on the Minnesota 18-yard line and converted for a 7-0 lead heading into halftime. In the second half, Spears decided to put his trust in the considerable talents of his defense, hoping it could wear down the Fighting Irish offense. He decided to punt frequently on first and second down in an effort to win the battle of field position. This tactic was aided by the spectacular punting of Harold Barnhart, who averaged 51 yards per kick.

Late in the contest, Nagurski broke through the line on defense, crashed into the punter and recovered the ball on the Notre Dame 15. On fourth down, Joesting hit Leonard Walsh with a scoring pass to pull the Gophers to within 7-6, setting up the crucial extra-point try for the tie, much the same as the Michigan game in 1903. And just as Ed Rogers converted in that classic, Art Pharmer did his part 24 years later.

A Title Turned Down

The unlikely tie with Notre Dame kept the undefeated season alive. The following week, the Gophers downed Drake 27-6, and in the season finale, 10,000 fans made the trip to Michigan — joining some 75,000 Wolverine boosters — to watch the visitors reclaim the Little Brown Jug 13-7.

Minnesota finished its magical season 6-0-2 overall and 3-0-1 in the Big Ten, with both an undefeated season and a share of the title — at least on paper — for the first time since 1915. However, President Coffman declined an official claim to a share of the championship, saying his men could be content with "the fine reputation they had achieved."

Joesting was named All-American for a second straight year and was joined on

MINNESOTA 7, NOTRE DAME 7

10 BIG GAMES REMEMBERED: 1922-1931

Nov. 5, 1927: Minnesota 7, Notre Dame 7, in South Bend. The Fighting Irish hadn't lost in South Bend since 1905. Notre Dame held the lead most of the game, but Bronislav "Bronko" Nagurski came to the rescue by breaking through the line and crashing into the Notre Dame punter to cause a fumble he recovered deep in Irish territory. Herb Joesting passed to Leonard Walsh to make it 7-6, and Art Pharmer calmly converted the kick for the tie.

10 BIG GAMES REMEMBERED: 1922-1931

Nov. 24, 1928: Minnesota 6, Wisconsin 0, in Madison. The Gophers ended the Big Ten title hopes of the Badgers behind an amazing performance by Bronko Nagurski. Nagurski recovered a fumble at the Wisconsin 17 and plowed in six plays later for the game's only score. He later stopped Bo Cuisinier in the open field, knocked down a key fourth-down pass at the Minnesota 4-yard line and intercepted a last-ditch Wisconsin pass as time expired.

(Top) The Gophers stuff a Notre Dame ball carrier during the 1927 game that ended in a 7-7 tie. The Fighting Irish had not lost — or been tied — at home since 1905. (Inset left) Bronko Nagurski is the only player to be named All-America on both offense and defense in the same season. (Above) Nagurski plows for yardage against Wisconsin. His coach in the pros, George Halas of the Chicago Bears, said Nagurski was "virtually unstoppable" as "the best fullback I ever saw."

The Associated Press team by Hanson.

Nagurski took over for Joesting at fullback in 1928, but nag[...] injuries — and only for Bronko could you call broken bones in his [...] "nagging injuries" — kept him from playing the position full time, a[...] that no doubt had opposing defenses rejoicing at their good fortun[...] such luck for the offenses, however, as Nagurski was still able to an[...] the bell and wreak havoc at defensive tackle.

The Gophers' talent was again strong, with Hovde stepping [...] fullback, All-American Ken Haycraft and Bob Tanner at ends and cap[...] George Gibson at guard.

Gibson was a powerful blocker, a stopper on defense and w[...] also go on to be an All-America[...] addition, he was Nagurski's S[...] Chi fraternity roommate. The [...] was that Gibson used to be ab[...] outwrestle Nagurski, which m[...] a person wonder how st[...] Gibson was.

As good as the Gophers [...] in 1928 and again the follo[...] year, they were beset by [...] narrow losses that cost the[...] chance at a championship. In 1[...] they lost 7-6 to Iowa and 10-[...] Northwestern, and in 1929 [...] were beaten 9-7 by Iowa and [...] by Michigan.

The Nagurski legend h[...] zenith in the final game of 1[...]

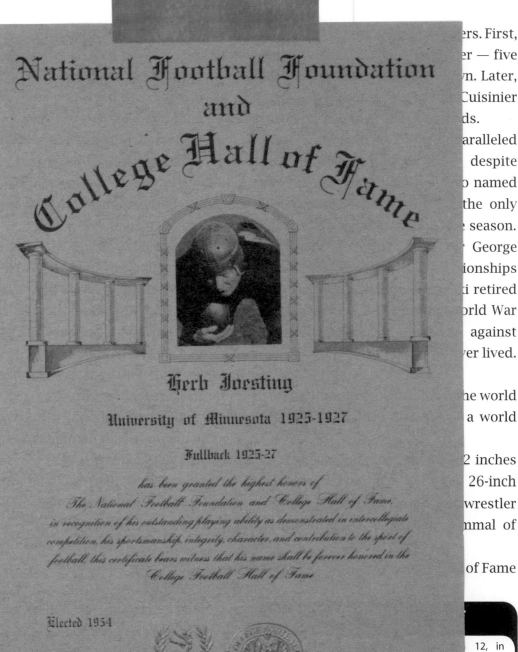

(Inset) Herb Joesting, the "Owatonna Thunderbolt," helped bring home the Little Brown Jug from Ann Arbor in 1927, the first time the Gophers had beaten Michigan for the jug since 1919. (Below) Games w[...] traditional rivals drew capacity crowds. In 1929, more than 58,000 packed the stadium for the Michigan and Wisconsin games.

[...] 12, in [...] coach [...] Wisconsin [...]ed by Art Pharmer and Bronko Nagurski, who were playing their last games for the maroon and gold. Nagurski scored both touchdowns on runs of 1 and 3 yards, while Pharmer kicked the extra point following the first touchdown and added a 43-yard run to set up the second score.

America voted to name the annual award for college football's top defensive player the Bronko Nagurski Trophy.

He remains one of the state's most beloved almost-native sons. In 1938 he was named Minnesota's all-time outstanding athlete by the *St. Paul Dispatch-Pioneer Press*, and 62 years later he was chosen the second-greatest Minnesota sportsman of the century, trailing only the iconic baseball hero Kirby Puckett of the Minnesota Twins.

When his career was over, Nagurski returned to International Falls and ran both a farm and a gas station, allegedly screwing on gas caps so tight that you needed a wrench to get them off. Pages more could be written about this giant of a man, and for the insatiable appetite, there is a fix available — the Bronko Nagurski Museum in International Falls, one of the few museums in America devoted to a single player.

HE SHOULD HAVE BEEN IN PICTURES

Despite five straight winning seasons, a cumulative record of 28-9-3 and a slew of narrow defeats in his final two seasons, Spears was finding it tough to please the legions of Gophers fans who craved nothing less than conference championships. After the 1929 season, Spears resigned for a coaching job at the University of Oregon.

His successor was Herbert O. "Fritz" Crisler, who was hired as both head football coach and athletic director. The move raised the eyebrows of more than a few Gophers backers since Crisler came to town with no head coaching experience. He had, however, been a player and an assistant at the University of Chicago under Amos Alonzo Stagg, and he chose a number of familiar names to be his assistants: Sig Harris, Bert Baston and Frank McCormick.

While the hire itself befuddled some, Crisler's style had others, including players, scratching their heads. Crisler was low key, averse to profanity, one whom university historian James Gray described as "a moving picture studio version of the football coach as hero. Handsome, suave, socially gifted, he brought to the gridiron some of the graces of the drawing room and this seemed so fantastic to some of his more earthy players that it cost him their faith in his method. More used to being cursed in all high-hearted joviality than to being paid the compliments which a diplomat might frame, they felt in the dressing room a breath, neither cold nor warm, of the utterly unfamiliar."

Despite his lack of top-dog coaching pedigree, Crisler fielded two respectable teams. The 1930 version went 3-4-1 but could muster only one conference win, 6-0 against Indiana.

The following year brought considerably more success — a 7-3 record that included a season-ending 19-7 victory against Ohio State in a postseason charity game that dashed the Buckeyes' title hopes.

A large figure in these years was Clarence "Biggie" Munn of Minneapolis, who began his career as a sophomore blocking for Nagurski. At 220 pounds, he was an agile two-way player. As a defensive lineman, he was

(Below) A pass is up for grabs between a Minnesota receiver and an Ohio State defender, in white, during a 1931 charity game that ended in a 19-7 Gophers victory. It was played for the benefit of the unemployed during the Great Depression, and it was an unusual matchup. Despite being in the same conference for nearly 20 years, the two teams had met only twice previously.

10 BIG GAMES REMEMBERED: 1922-1931

Nov. 28, 1931: Minnesota 19, Ohio State 7, in Minneapolis. The Gophers unleashed a full arsenal of weapons against the Buckeyes in a postseason game played for the benefit of the unemployed. Clarence "Biggie" Munn, Jack Manders and Pete Somers were the stars for Minnesota. The All-American Munn opened huge holes all day, and also threw two passes and ran a few times. Manders rushed for 130 yards and a touchdown, and Somers also scored.

THE GOLDEN YEARS

Given Bierman's penchant for power and precision blocking, the single wing was a match made in football heaven.

ernie Bierman first arrived on Minnesota's campus as a player in 1912, a homegrown kid who was born on a farm near Springfield and grew up in Litchfield. As a youth he struggled with a bum leg — the result of a bone infection — and it took several operations before he was able to participate in sports.

But participate he did, and athletics would eventually define his life. At Litchfield High School, Bierman excelled in football, basketball, baseball and track, and he decided to bring his multi-sport talents to the University of Minnesota to play for Henry "Doc" Williams. He became an All-America halfback — in addition to playing basketball and running track — and captained the unbeaten 1915 team that won the conference title.

After leaving the university, Bierman coached high school football for a year in Montana before enlisting in the Marine Corps, where he was commissioned a captain. After World War I, it was back into football, with head coaching stints at Montana, Mississippi A&M and Tulane.

Success followed Bierman at every step of his coaching journey, and in his last year at Tulane — where his overall record was 36-10-1 — he took the Green Wave to the Rose Bowl.

So, it was no surprise Bierman was brought home to lead his alma mater, and with Frank McCormick assuming the role of athletic director, Bierman could focus on football.

Nicknamed "The Grey Eagle," Bierman was a relentless taskmaster and a perfectionist, which meant long hours on the practice field, endless repetitions of plays and conditioning that would make a Marine proud.

CALL HIM "PUG"

His bread-and-butter was the single-wing offense, the poster child of midcentury power football. Given Bierman's penchant for power and precision blocking, the single wing was a match made in football heaven.

All of Bierman's preparation found mixed success at first. In 1932 the Gophers put together a decent record of 5-3, but they were only 2-3 in the Big Ten, with losses to Purdue, Wisconsin and, in the season finale, Michigan. The 3-0 loss Nov. 19 to the Wolverines would be a watershed date for the Gophers, as they would go nearly four years before suffering another loss.

A key figure in Bierman's first campaign was Francis Lund from Rice Lake, Wisconsin. Early in his career, Lund acquired a more macho nickname. As the story goes, he was chatting with a reporter from the *Minneapolis Star*

1932-1950

(Preceding page) Minnesota's equipment managers go over inventory in 1937. The cleats on the shoes hanging from the ceiling were three-quarters of an inch. In 1970, the rule was changed to one-half inch cleats. (Right) A young Bernie Bierman after he was hired in 1932 to coach his alma mater. Bierman would coach the Gophers for 16 of the next 19 years, with time out for World War II.

(Below) Bob Tenner is tackled in the end zone after catching a pass from Francis "Pug" Lund. The touchdown was the difference in a 7-3 victory over Pitt in the early stages of a 28-game unbeaten streak. (Below left) Four members of that 1933 team — John Roning, Ellsworth Harpole, Stan Lundgren and Carl Tengler — are featured over an artist's version of the win over Pitt.

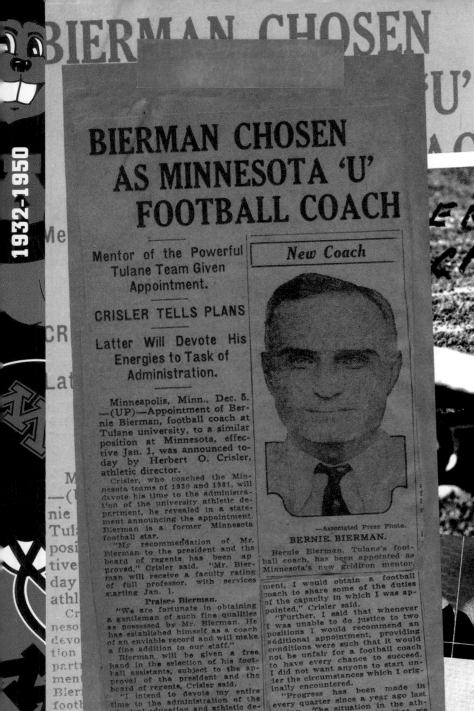

BIERMAN CHOSEN AS MINNESOTA 'U' FOOTBALL COACH

Mentor of the Powerful Tulane Team Given Appointment.

CRISLER TELLS PLANS

Latter Will Devote His Energies to Task of Administration.

New Coach

BERNIE BIERMAN.

Bernie Bierman, Tulane's football coach, has been appointed as Minnesota's new gridiron mentor.

Minneapolis, Minn., Dec. 5. —(UP)—Appointment of Bernie Bierman, football coach at Tulane university, to a similar position at Minnesota, effective Jan. 1, was announced today by Herbert O. Crisler, athletic director.

Crisler, who coached the Minnesota teams of 1930 and 1931, will devote his time to the administration of the university athletic department, he revealed in a statement announcing the appointment. Bierman is a former Minnesota football star.

"My recommendation of Mr. Bierman to the president and the board of regents has been approved," Crisler said. "Mr. Bierman will receive a faculty rating of full professor, with services starting Jan. 1.

Praises Bierman.

"We are fortunate in obtaining a gentleman of such fine qualities as possessed by Mr. Bierman. He has established himself as a coach of an enviable record and will make a fine addition to our staff."

Bierman will be given a free hand in the selection of his football assistants, subject to the approval of the president and the board of regents, Crisler said.

"I intend to devote my entire time to the administration of the physical education and athletic department," Crisler said. "It will be my objective to inject the same spirit into all our athletics that has been so abundant in our recent football teams."

Recalls Statement.

"Last year I made the statement that whenever in my opinion I felt it was for the best interest of the university and the athletic department, I would obtain a football coach to share some of the duties of the capacity in which I was appointed," Crisler said.

"Further, I said that whenever I was unable to do justice to two positions I would recommend an additional appointment, providing conditions were such that it would not be unfair for a football coach to have every chance to succeed. I did not want anyone to start under the circumstances which I originally encountered.

"Progress has been made in every quarter since a year ago last spring. The situation in the athletic department is such that we can look to the future with considerable hope as a result of the foundations which have been securely built. The urge of matters in connection with the department is such that considerable time is demanded to carry to a conclusion a successful administration."

—Associated Press Photo.

TENGLER

10 BIG GAMES REMEMBERED: 1932-1950

Oct. 21, 1933: Minnesota 7, Pittsburgh 3, in Minneapolis. Pitt was coming off a trip to the Rose Bowl, but the Gophers were ready for the strong Panthers. Minnesota scored on some trickery late in the first quarter when Francis "Pug" Lund took the snap, started to run forward but stopped short of the line of scrimmage, then faked a pass downfield and delivered a shovel pass to Bob Tenner, whose 15-yard touchdown run held up for the Gophers' victory.

while posing for pictures when the reporter asked him his name, to which he replied, "Francis Lund."

"Francis. That's a hell of a name for a football player," said the reporter. "Don't you have a nickname?"

There was silence from Lund, but a teammate chimed in, "Why don't you call him Pug?"

When a caption under a publicity photo in the newspaper the next day read, "Pug Lund legs it," the name stuck like a growling dog to a postman's pants.

Bierman's second campaign in 1933 was the ultimate transition season. A number of new players would become catalysts for future greatness: Julius Alfonse, Sheldon Beise, Babe LeVoir, Glen Seidel and Dick Smith. And Bill Bevan and George Svendsen arrived in Minnesota after a year in Oregon playing for former Gophers coach Clarence "Doc" Spears.

Minnesota arrived on the field that year wearing gold from head to toe. It wasn't the bright gold of today but rather a mustard gold — "old gold" on some palettes. The new look inspired the iconic, cigar-chomping broadcaster Halsey Hall to announce, "Here come the Golden Gophers!" and a new nickname entered the vocabulary.

The Golden Gophers were very good, especially on defense, surrendering a total of only 32 points and never more than a single touchdown in a game. But they had trouble offensively, scoring only 64 points and playing to scoreless ties against Northwestern and Michigan.

Greatness Is Tapped

The breakthrough game occurred in week four when Minnesota played powerful Pitt, which was coming off a Rose Bowl appearance the previous season. Late in the first quarter at Memorial Stadium, Minnesota scored on some trickery. Lund took the snap and started to run forward but stopped short of the line. There he faked a pass downfield and instead delivered a shovel pass to Bob Tenner, who was running left to right along the line. Tenner's 15-yard score held up for a 7-3 Gopher victory.

A 6-3 win over Wisconsin in the season finale gave Minnesota a 4-0-4 record, good for a share of the Big Ten title. Greatness had been tapped, and it was about to flow in a torrent.

Some new additions for 1934 were the final pieces in the puzzle: fullback Stan Kostka, halfback Art Clarkson and stalwart linemen Ed Widseth, Bud Wilkinson and Red Oech. Minnesota was two deep at virtually every position and poised for a big run.

After routing North Dakota State 56-12 to open the season, the Golden Gophers downed Nebraska 20-0. That set up an encore matchup at Pitt, a game that would define the season.

Bierman's strategy that day harked back to a tactic used by Spears and Doc Williams — punting early and letting the defense wear the opponent down. Against Pitt, the Gophers punted on second down most of the game. At halftime, Minnesota trailed 7-0, but Bierman stuck with the strategy, and it finally paid off.

(Above right) End Butch Larson and halfback Lund were both two-time All-Americans in 1933-34. Guard Bill Bevan and end Tenner joined them on the '34 All-America squad. (Right) Lund, left, the '34 captain-elect, accepts the torch from the 1933 leader, center Roy Oen. The ceremony was a tradition at the end of every season.

1932-1950

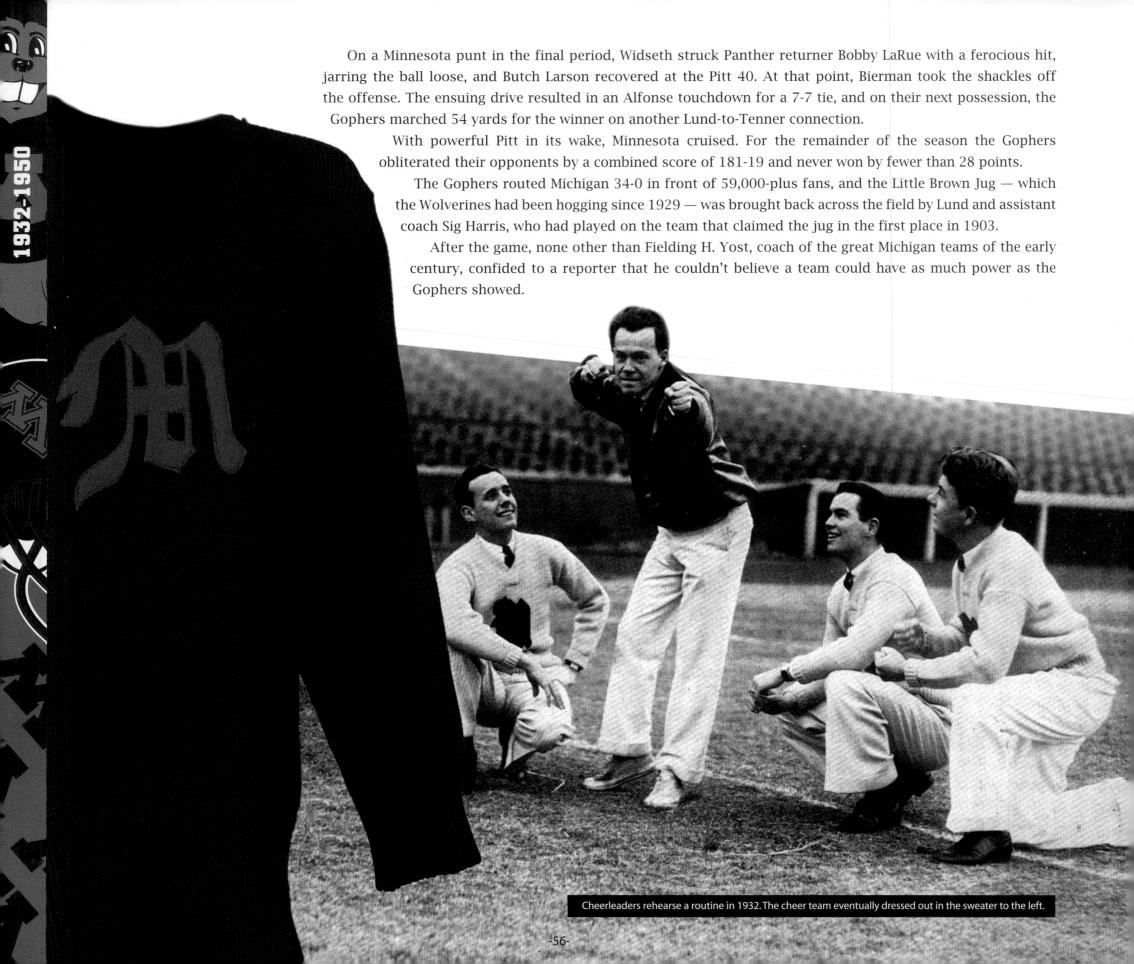

On a Minnesota punt in the final period, Widseth struck Panther returner Bobby LaRue with a ferocious hit, jarring the ball loose, and Butch Larson recovered at the Pitt 40. At that point, Bierman took the shackles off the offense. The ensuing drive resulted in an Alfonse touchdown for a 7-7 tie, and on their next possession, the Gophers marched 54 yards for the winner on another Lund-to-Tenner connection.

With powerful Pitt in its wake, Minnesota cruised. For the remainder of the season the Gophers obliterated their opponents by a combined score of 181-19 and never won by fewer than 28 points.

The Gophers routed Michigan 34-0 in front of 59,000-plus fans, and the Little Brown Jug — which the Wolverines had been hogging since 1929 — was brought back across the field by Lund and assistant coach Sig Harris, who had played on the team that claimed the jug in the first place in 1903.

After the game, none other than Fielding H. Yost, coach of the great Michigan teams of the early century, confided to a reporter that he couldn't believe a team could have as much power as the Gophers showed.

Cheerleaders rehearse a routine in 1932. The cheer team eventually dressed out in the sweater to the left.

THE FIRST CHAMPIONSHIP

Minnesota finished the job with another 34-0 pasting of Wisconsin in Madison. Lund started the rout with touchdowns of 2 and 59 yards and would go on to gain 150 yards on just 12 carries. At about the same time, the Gophers learned Indiana had beaten Purdue — the only other unbeaten Big Ten team — 13-7.

The lead paragraph in the following day's *Minneapolis Sunday Tribune* proclaimed the news: "Complementing crushing power with a display of Houdini magic that confounded the most physically stubborn defense they have met this season, the Gophers galloped roughshod over Wisconsin, 34 to 0, on soggy Camp Randall field Saturday to win the undisputed Big Ten football title and the national championship by general acclaim."

The deep, star-studded Gophers were national champions for the first time and boasted four All-America selections — Lund, Larson, Tenner and Bevan.

Bevan was the last player in the Big Ten to take the field without headgear. But apparently that put him at no competitive disadvantage, either physically or mentally. Said Bierman once of Bevan: "He never hit his stride until he was hit in the face."

(Right) Glenn Seidel was the quarterback and captain of 1935 team but broke his collarbone in the third game and was lost for the season. Despite the loss of Seidel and other significant departures, Minnesota went 8-0 and won its second straight national crown. (Below) Seidel signals a first down as Lund gets some tough yards against Pitt in '34. Tackle Phil Bengston, right, made All-Big Ten and later was the successor to Vince Lombardi as the coach of the Green Bay Packers in the NFL. (Bottom right) Ed Widseth's College Hall of Fame certificate. Seven Gophers players from the Bierman golden era were eventually selected to the College Hall of Fame. The coach was inducted in 1955.

National Football Foundation and College Hall of Fame

Ed Widseth

University of Minnesota 1934-1936

Tackle 1934-36

has been granted the highest honors of

10 BIG GAMES REMEMBERED: 1932-1950

Oct. 20, 1934: Minnesota 13, Pittsburgh 7, in Pittsburgh. In a critical game that helped them gain their first national title, the Gophers snuck past Pitt. For most of the game, Bernie Bierman relied on his stout defense by punting on second down. In the second half, Ed Widseth unloaded on Pitt punt returner Bobby LaRue, causing a fumble that was recovered at the Pitt 40. The Gophers responded with touchdowns by Julius Alfonse and Bob Tenner.

TENNER   LUND   BENGTSON   LARSON   WEINSTOCK   SEIDEL

1932-1950

1934 HOME COMING

LUND

SIG HARRIS

BIERMAN

MINN
MICH →

Lund RECIEVES Little Brown Jug from Michigan

Lund, Bierman and assistant coach Sig Harris cradle the Little Brown Jug after ending an eight-year drought against Michigan in 1934. Harris was a player on the 1903 team that claimed the jug in the first place.

Bringing Home The Bacon

Though it is odd to say, 1935 was something of a rebuilding year for Bierman. Lund and Larson were gone, along with other key players. Then the Big Ten made a change to its transfer rule, which ended the college careers of Kostka, Bevan, Clarkson and Svendsen, all of whom had transferred from Oregon. To make things even worse, Alfonse was academically ineligible.

Bierman would need to call on every bit of his depth and then hope the rest of the players would fill in the gaps. They answered the call.

The Gophers actually sputtered out of the gate, defeating North Dakota State 26-6 on the strength of two late touchdown passes by George Roscoe. A road game was next at Nebraska, and while Minnesota prevailed 12-7, it took a goal-line stand in the fourth quarter to preserve the victory. Roscoe scored both touchdowns, but his fumble deep in Minnesota territory necessitated the defensive heroics.

In the final non-conference tuneup against Tulane, quarterback and captain Seidel broke his collarbone and was lost for the season. No matter, because Minnesota's talented athletes took over and gained momentum as the season wore on. Northwestern was stopped 21-13, and Purdue fell 29-7.

That brought up a road contest at Iowa, and for some Iowans it stirred up bitter memories from the previous year when they thought Minnesota had unduly roughed up their star, Ozzie Simmons. Iowa Gov. Clyde Herring went so far as to suggest that "... if the officials stand for any rough tactics like Minnesota used last year, I'm sure the crowd will not."

Perhaps it was not the most diplomatic remark, but fortunately, Minnesota's beloved Gov. Floyd B. Olson conjured up a brilliant red herring. He suggested a light-hearted wager: A prized Minnesota hog would go to Iowa if the Hawkeyes won, and Iowa would pay up in pork if the Gophers won.

Herring took the bet, and at the end of the day, thanks to a 13-6 win, Minnesota brought home the bacon. The pig came from Rosedale Farms in Fort Dodge, Iowa, and was dubbed "Floyd of Rosedale" after the governor. Another of Minnesota's great trophy rivalry games was born. A bronze statue of a hog — still named Floyd of Rosedale — was sculpted by Minnesotan Charles Brioschi, and the winner of the annual battle gains the bragging and display rights to Floyd.

10 BIG GAMES REMEMBERED:
1932-1950

Nov. 24, 1934: Minnesota 34, Wisconsin 0, in Madison. It was only fitting that Minnesota claimed its first-ever national championship on the strength of a season-ending drubbing of longtime rival Wisconsin. All-American Francis "Pug" Lund led the Gopher charge, rushing for the first two touchdowns and 150 yards before leaving with an injury. Minnesota's defense picked off the Badgers seven times.

The 1934 team won the first of three straight national championships for Minnesota, a feat that has not been matched in college football. The Gophers added two more titles in 1940 and 1941, and another in 1960.

The following two weeks, the Gophers crushed Michigan 40-0 in Ann Arbor and Wisconsin at home 33-7 in the finale. With a perfect 8-0 record for the second straight year, the Gophers took a share of the Big Ten title and again were voted national champions.

Wilkinson, who played guard in 1935, tackles Dick Smith and Widseth and halfback Beise all were named to All-America teams.

With a 17-game winning streak on the line, another title run looked to be even more challenging in 1936, especially since Minnesota had replaced North Dakota State and Tulane on the non-conference schedule with Washington and Texas.

The season began with a four-day train trip to Seattle to play the Huskies, and Bierman had scheduled two practices for the Gophers along the way in Miles City, Montana, and Spokane. But the team almost never made it to Washington.

"IF YOU'RE A SUB, JUMP!"

At 3 a.m. Thursday, with the team asleep at the Florence Hotel in Missoula, a fire broke out in the drug store adjacent to the hotel. Fortunately, Ed Shave, the sports editor for the *St. Paul Daily News*, was up and about after an evening on the town when the fire broke out, and he alerted the desk clerk.

Assistant coach Bert Baston led the evacuation efforts, taking roll call of the team outside to ensure everyone was out and safe, and going inside one last time through the smoke to grab the last player. No one was hurt, but the hotel was destroyed, and the Gophers were fortunate to be able to head back to the train with team intact.

As time passed, the fire was fodder for many a Bierman story. In James Quirk's self-published volume of the early Bierman years, one yarn was recounted by a wire service scribe:

"At the meeting of the Pacific Coast coaches the other day, Bernie Bierman was the guest and told the best story. While en route to play Washington, the Gophers stopped overnight in Missoula, Montana. Fire broke out in the hotel during the night. Flames were shooting all around and some of the gridders couldn't decide what to do. 'Shall we jump for it or try the fire escape?' one of them yelled. Through the smoke the answer came back: 'If you are subs, go ahead and jump; regulars, use the fire escape!'"

The Gophers narrowly escaped Washington that weekend. The teams were locked in a 7-7 battle, each having scored after fumble recoveries. Then Alfonse and Wilkinson took over on defense. Alfonse intercepted three passes, and Wilkinson added another on the Minnesota 5-yard line. After recovering a fumble on the Washington 30, the Gophers finally converted for the go-ahead score in a 14-7 win.

Coming home to face Nebraska proved to be no picnic, either. Locked in a scoreless duel, the Cornhuskers held the Gophers on a goal-line stand late in the game. But the Gophers capitalized on a long, spectacular punt return, with Wilkinson lateraling to Andy Uram on a play covering 78 yards as Minnesota won 7-0.

Of the spectacular broken-field run, Bierman noted that at one point or another, every Nebraska player was on the ground, and he would later say, "It was the only play I've seen which arose spontaneously and reflected perfection in every detail." Coming from a perfectionist, that is high praise indeed.

(Opposite pa
Dr. George Ha
World War

10 BIG GAMES REMEMBERED:
1932-1950

Nov. 9, 1935: Minnesota 13, Iowa 6, in Iowa City. One of the Gophers' spirited trophy rivalries was born this day in an emotionally charged game with the Iowa Hawkeyes. Minnesota Gov. Floyd B. Olson had diffused some bad blood between the teams by proposing a friendly wager with his counterpart: To the victor of the contest would go a prized hog, courtesy of the losers. Minnesota won the pig, which went on to become the Floyd of Rosedale trophy.

MINNESOTA
NATIONAL FOOTBALL CHAMPION
1935
PRESENTED BY
NATIONAL ITALIAN AMERICAN

1932-1950

(Above) A Minnesota player is helped from the Florence Hotel in Missoula, Montana, after a fire broke out. The team was on its way to Washington for a game against the Huskies and had been staying overnight in Missoula after practicing. No one was injured in the fire. (Right) The Gophers finally made it to Seattle and pulled out a 14-7 victory in the first game of their march to the 1936 championship — the first to be awarded by The Associated Press.

THE FIRST AP CHAMP

Bierman's machine kicked it into gear the following two weeks, drubbing Michigan 26-0 and Purdue 33-0. This was the year The Associated Press began its weekly rankings, and the Gophers entered the game against Purdue ranked No. 1. They carried that ranking the following week into a pivotal matchup at No. 3 Northwestern.

In the mud in Evanston, the Gophers had plenty of chances to score but couldn't make the mark, and the Wildcats prevailed 6-0, thus ending the Gophers' 28-game unbeaten streak and, seemingly, their title hopes.

Minnesota scored plenty the last three weeks of the season, beating Iowa 52-0, Texas 47-19 and Wisconsin 24-0. The Gophers finished the season 7-1 overall and 4-1 in the Big Ten, good for a tie for second in the conference.

Ultimately, it would be good enough for even more. Northwestern wound up losing its season finale to Notre Dame 26-0, and the AP voted Minnesota the national champion for 1936.

More than a half-century before the term would be coined, the Gophers had pulled off an unexpected and unprecedented three-peat.

Two narrow defeats in 1937 — 14-9 at Nebraska and 7-6 at home to Notre Dame — were all that stood between the Gophers and another undefeated season, and those two losses were twice as many as they had suffered in the previous four years combined. If it was any consolation — and for a perfectionist like Bierman, it certainly wasn't — the Gophers ran the table in the Big Ten for another conference championship. They finished the season ranked No. 5, and Ray King and Uram were named All-Americans.

The Gophers again finished 6-2 in 1938 and flirted briefly with the prospect of a national title. They began the season 4-0 and took a No. 2 ranking into a late-October game at Northwestern. Once again, the Wildcats put a lid on Minnesota's momentum and dealt the visitors a 6-3 setback.

(Right) "A Cradle of Coaches" is pictured, as Bengston, bottom, coached the Packers in the NFL; Milt Bruhn, center, coached Wisconsin to two Rose Bowls in 11 seasons; and Bud Wilkinson became a College Football Hall of Fame coach at Oklahoma. Wilkinson's teams had a 47-game winning streak, a record for major colleges. He was also an All-America guard at Minnesota. (Below) Andy Uram sets sail on his punt return — after a lateral from Wilkinson — that beat Nebraska in 1936.

TALES OF THE CORNHUSKERS

NEBRASKA
MINNESOTA

MEMORIAL STADIUM OCT. 12

**10 BIG GAMES REMEMBERED:
1932-1950**

Oct. 10, 1936: Minnesota 7, Nebraska 0, in Minneapolis. When the Cornhuskers held Minnesota on a goal-line stand late in the game, it looked as if a scoreless tie was inevitable. Then Bud Wilkinson dropped back to field a short punt with just over a minute remaining. As Wilkinson was being tackled, he used a lateral to a beckoning Andy Uram, who raced 78 yards to paydirt. The victory pushed the Gophers' winning streak to 19 games.

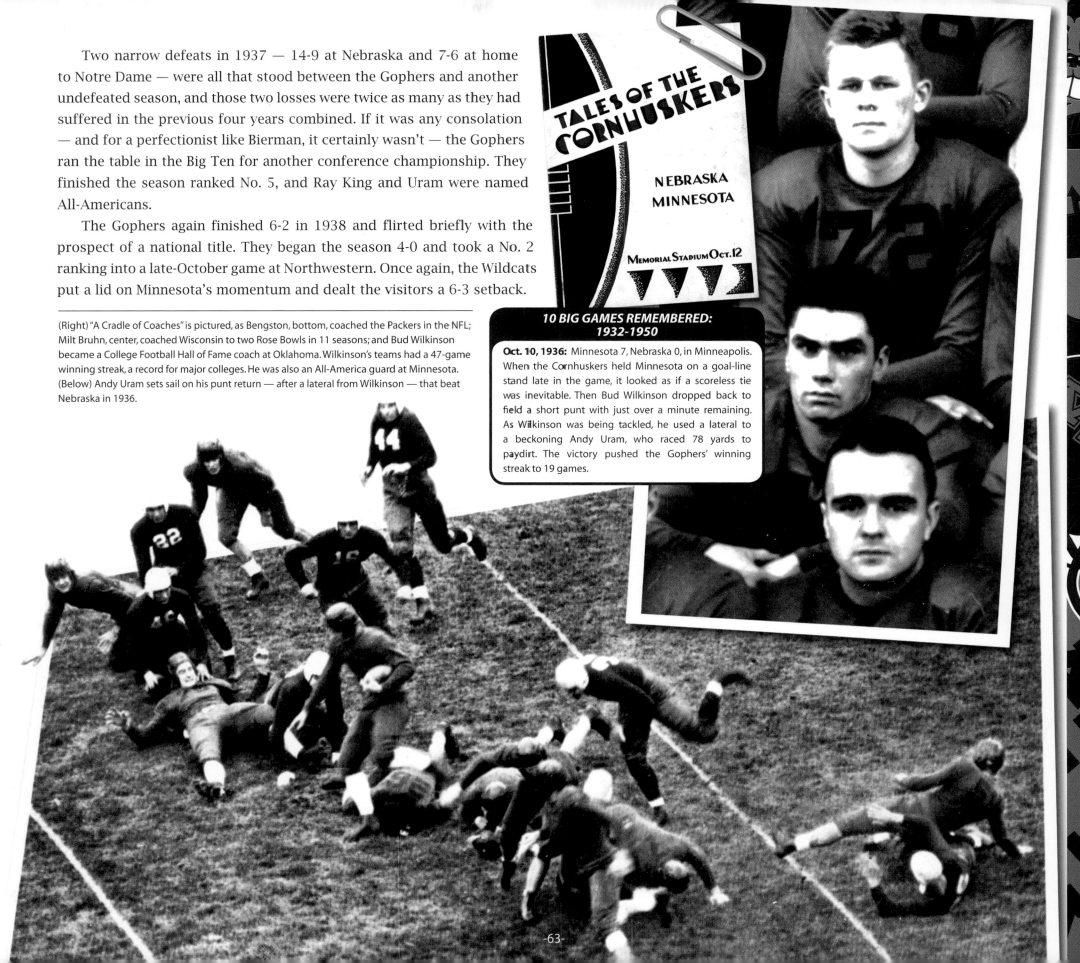

1932-1950

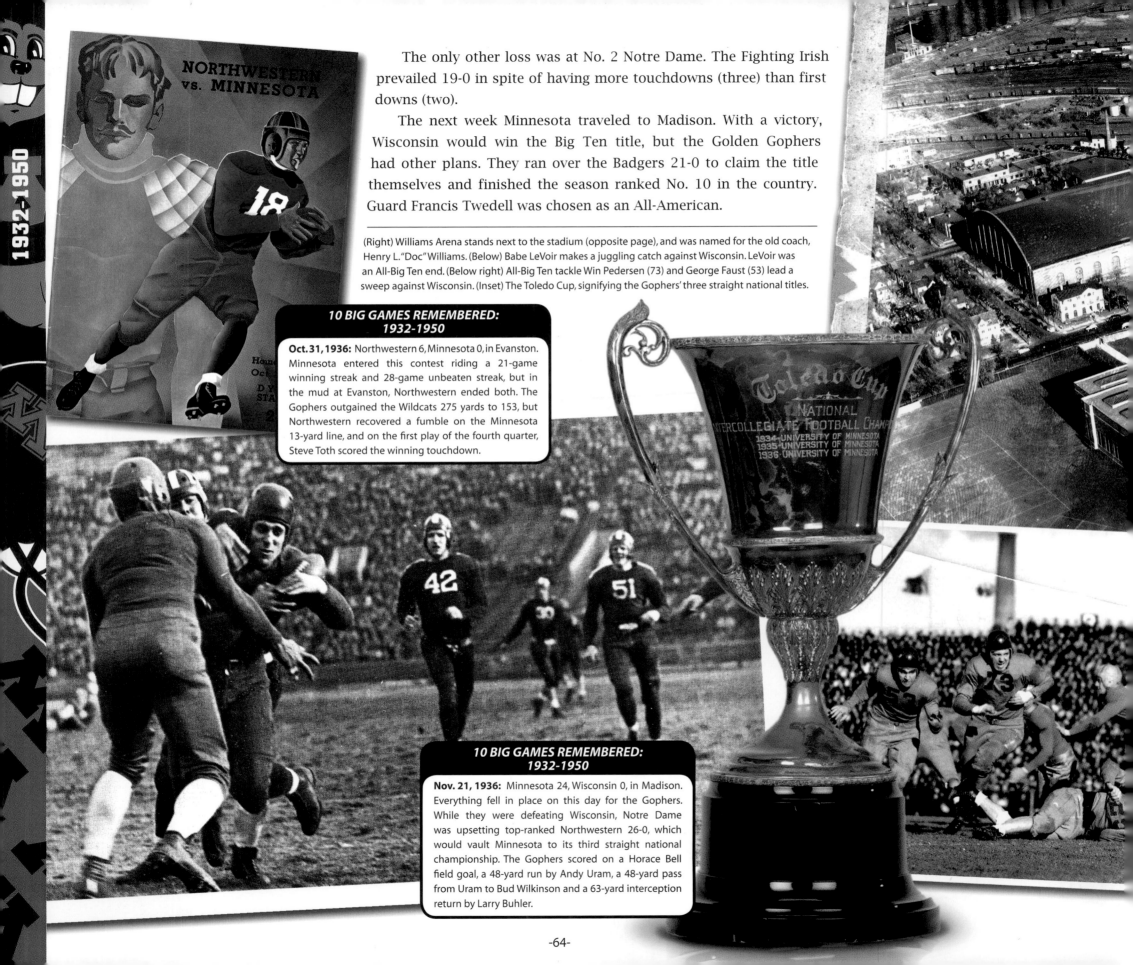

NORTHWESTERN vs. MINNESOTA

18

Houe...
Oc...
D.Y...
STA...
2...

The only other loss was at No. 2 Notre Dame. The Fighting Irish prevailed 19-0 in spite of having more touchdowns (three) than first downs (two).

The next week Minnesota traveled to Madison. With a victory, Wisconsin would win the Big Ten title, but the Golden Gophers had other plans. They ran over the Badgers 21-0 to claim the title themselves and finished the season ranked No. 10 in the country. Guard Francis Twedell was chosen as an All-American.

(Right) Williams Arena stands next to the stadium (opposite page), and was named for the old coach, Henry L. "Doc" Williams. (Below) Babe LeVoir makes a juggling catch against Wisconsin. LeVoir was an All-Big Ten end. (Below right) All-Big Ten tackle Win Pedersen (73) and George Faust (53) lead a sweep against Wisconsin. (Inset) The Toledo Cup, signifying the Gophers' three straight national titles.

10 BIG GAMES REMEMBERED: 1932-1950

Oct. 31, 1936: Northwestern 6, Minnesota 0, in Evanston. Minnesota entered this contest riding a 21-game winning streak and 28-game unbeaten streak, but in the mud at Evanston, Northwestern ended both. The Gophers outgained the Wildcats 275 yards to 153, but Northwestern recovered a fumble on the Minnesota 13-yard line, and on the first play of the fourth quarter, Steve Toth scored the winning touchdown.

10 BIG GAMES REMEMBERED: 1932-1950

Nov. 21, 1936: Minnesota 24, Wisconsin 0, in Madison. Everything fell in place on this day for the Gophers. While they were defeating Wisconsin, Notre Dame was upsetting top-ranked Northwestern 26-0, which would vault Minnesota to its third straight national championship. The Gophers scored on a Horace Bell field goal, a 48-yard run by Andy Uram, a 48-yard pass from Uram to Bud Wilkinson and a 63-yard interception return by Larry Buhler.

Toledo Cup
NATIONAL
INTERCOLLEGIATE FOOTBALL CHAMP...
1934-UNIVERSITY OF MINNESOTA
1935-UNIVERSITY OF MINNESOTA
1936-UNIVERSITY OF MINNESOTA

U. of M.
the
Home of the
GOPHER
GOPHERS

1938 FOOTBALL SCHEDULE

Sept. 24, Washington	Oct. 29, N.W. (at Evanston)
Oct. 1, Nebraska	Nov. 5, Iowa (Dad's Day)
Oct. 8, Purdue	Nov. 12, Notre Dame
Oct. 15, Michigan	(at Notre Dame)
(Homecoming)	Nov. 19, Wis. (at Madison)

PERINE'S
the
House of
USED TEXT
BOOKS

PERINE'S

Bierman coached five national champions at Minnesota — an unmatched feat — but never took the Gophers to a Rose Bowl. Big Ten rules prohibited it in the 1930s and early '40s.

(Above) The band forms the block "M" at halftime of a game in 1940. (Inset) Bruce Smith was Minnesota's first — and to date, only — Heisman Trophy winner in 1941. He even starred in a movie, "Smith of Minnesota," before going off to war.

Tickets are pri...
will be Dads Day...
Paffrath, George F...
Ed Steinbauer, Bill...

Tickets are priced...
of Minnesota-Wisc...

Under a rulin...
ference games is p...
and ushers have b...

The Ticket...
Articles found in...
Department. Ar...
Main 8101 or N...
are retained in th...
Department in th...

...FOUND DEPARTMENT

...and Found Department with the aid of the...
...anded to any Boy Scout for delivery to the Lost and...
...ands may be traced by calling the Football Ticket O...
...effort will be made to locate lost articles. Found arti...
...days. Thereafter, they will be sent to the Lost and Foun...
...Building of the University and should be called for there.

...Please retain your stub.

...um, use the ramp through which you entered.

...PASS-OUT CHECKS

When lea...

...ou to leave the Stadium during progress of the game and
If it becomes nece... ...you leave by the Pass-Out Gates which are numbers 3, 7,
you desire to return, b... ...ion to the gatemen and obtain from them a pass-out check.
11, 21, 24, 31. Indicate... ...ion to your ticket stub in order to re-enter the Stadium.
This check will be re...

It would be tempting t...
and technically it was. Th...
Bierman's tenure. But the...
and 13-9 — and the team...

NEW DECADE, N...

The start of a new decad...
brought a new cast of h...
a slew of talented backs...
Paffrath, Bob Sweiger and...

If luck was against t...
along with dashes of grit...
were come-from-behind e...
touchdown or less.

For most of the...
defensively. He s...
returned kickoffs...
and had a big hand in...
his defensive play.

However, the game th...
myth creator — came ag...
came to Memorial Stadiur...
played in the rain, which would do nothing to keep away a crowd of more

10 BIG GAMES REMEMBERED: 1932-1950

Nov. 9, 1940: Minnesota 7, Michigan 6, in Minneapolis. Third-ranked Michigan came to town to battle No. 2 Minnesota. The Gophers held star Tom Harmon and the Wolverines to only one touchdown, with Harmon missing the conversion. Then it was Bruce Smith's turn. After switching positions with George "Sonny" Franck, Smith took a Franck handoff on a reverse and galloped 80 yards through the mud for the tying touchdown, and Joseph Mernik's extra point won it.

(Above) A clash of the titans: Michigan's Tom Harmon, "Ol' 98," prepares to meet Bruce Smith in 1940, a game won by the Gophers on an 80-yard run by Smith and a missed extra point by Harmon, who won the Heisman Trophy that season. (Inset) Smith's Heisman Trophy, won the year after Harmon received the award.

than 60,000, but during the next couple of days, that rain would change into the Armistice Day Blizzard.

Michigan was led by the great running back Tom Harmon, who was on his way to winning the Heisman Trophy. The Wolverines threatened early and often, but Minnesota was up for the challenge. Twice Michigan drove inside the Minnesota 10-yard line, and both times they were stonewalled. Michigan finally hit "paymud" but had to go airborne, with Harmon hitting Forest Evashevski with a 2-yard pass. Harmon missed the conversion, which would come back to haunt him.

Moments later, Minnesota was forced to make another goal-line stand after Michigan blocked a Franck punt. That one was capped by an interception in the end zone by Paffrath. What happened next in the slop at University and Oak was one for the ages.

On first down, Smith switched positions with Franck, leaving the latter at left halfback while Smith took his spot on the right wing. Franck took the snap and ran right, then handed off to Smith on a reverse. Smith plied a hole off left tackle between blocks by Dick Wildung and Bill Kuusisto and headed upfield. Harmon was sealed off with a block. Evashevski made contact but couldn't hold on. Smith was off to the races, leaving a trail of mud and 11 Wolverines in his 80-yard wake. Joseph Mernik kicked the extra point and Minnesota held on to stymie Michigan 7-6.

Harmon later said of Smith's gallop, "It was the greatest run I ever saw and the greatest disappointment I ever suffered. Seven Michigan players had a shot at Smith on that run."

The victory vaulted the Gophers to No. 1 in the AP poll, and they closed out the season in fine fashion, downing Purdue 33-6 at home and beating

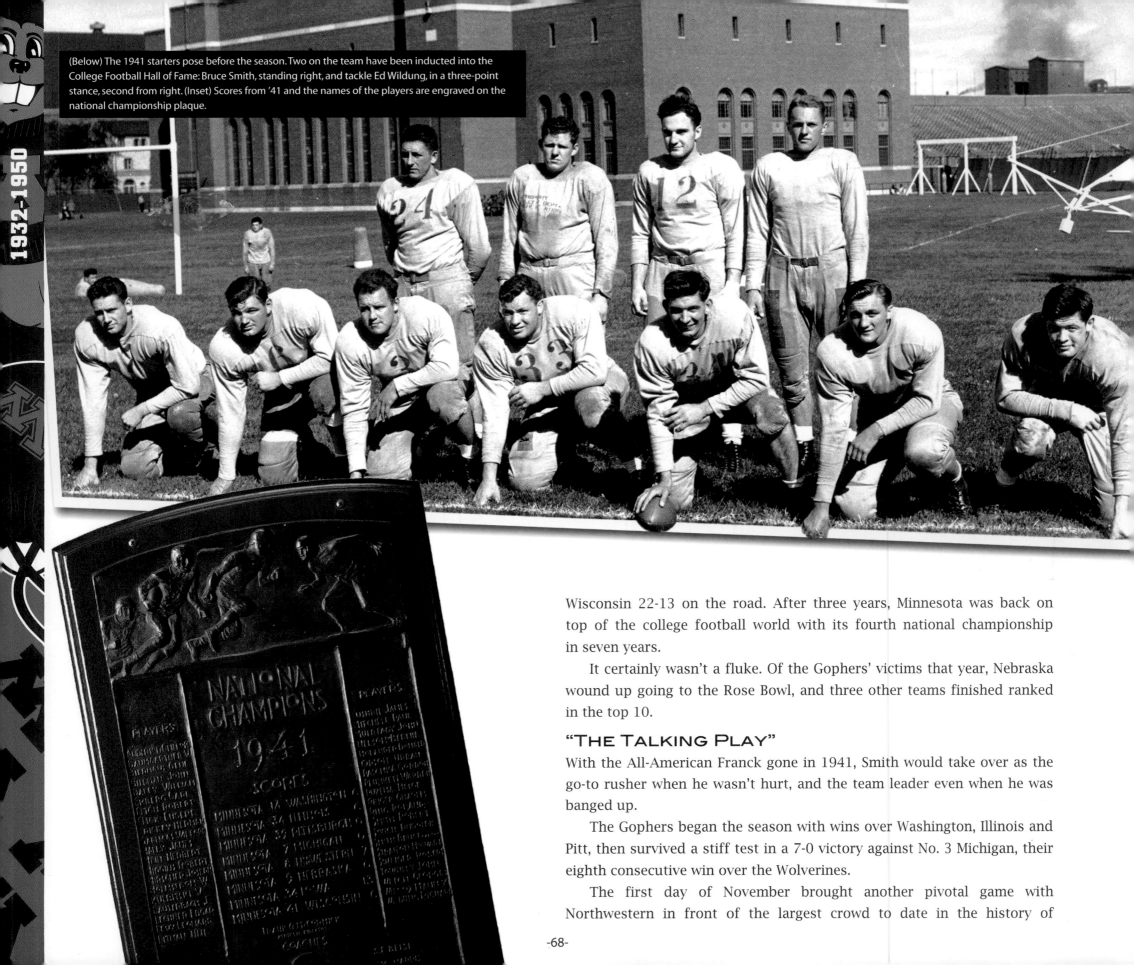

(Below) The 1941 starters pose before the season. Two on the team have been inducted into the College Football Hall of Fame: Bruce Smith, standing right, and tackle Ed Wildung, in a three-point stance, second from right. (Inset) Scores from '41 and the names of the players are engraved on the national championship plaque.

Wisconsin 22-13 on the road. After three years, Minnesota was back on top of the college football world with its fourth national championship in seven years.

It certainly wasn't a fluke. Of the Gophers' victims that year, Nebraska wound up going to the Rose Bowl, and three other teams finished ranked in the top 10.

"THE TALKING PLAY"

With the All-American Franck gone in 1941, Smith would take over as the go-to rusher when he wasn't hurt, and the team leader even when he was banged up.

The Gophers began the season with wins over Washington, Illinois and Pitt, then survived a stiff test in a 7-0 victory against No. 3 Michigan, their eighth consecutive win over the Wolverines.

The first day of November brought another pivotal game with Northwestern in front of the largest crowd to date in the history of

A TOAST TO BERNIE BIERMAN

WINNER OF
6 Big Ten - 4 National
FOOTBALL CHAMPIONSHIPS

at the ANNUAL

MINNESOTA FOOTBALL DINNER

FRIDAY, DEC. 5, 1941

ROOM   HUYLER'S,
310 SOUTH MICHIGAN

where previous dinners were held.)

...sotan:

...your calendar for December 5th, t...
...all loyal Minnesotans gather to...
...ast to the greatest football coac...
...land. Bernie Bierman, Dr. Hau...
...there.

10 BIG GAMES REMEMBERED: 1932-1950

Nov. 1, 1941: Minnesota 8, Northwestern 7, in Minneapolis. This was the famous "talking play" game. Minnesota was trailing the Wildcats 7-2, so, the day after Halloween, Bernie Bierman dipped into his bag of tricks. After running a reverse out of bounds on the left sideline, the Gopher linemen and backs casually took their places while chatting with the Northwestern players. Suddenly, center Gene Flick centered the ball to Bud Higgins, who sped down the field for the winning touchdown.

Memorial Stadium — 64,464. It was a crisp, cool afternoon, and the Wildcats were out to avenge their 13-12 loss a year earlier. Minnesota would need to throw everything at the Wildcats to prevail, including some well-timed skullduggery — courtesy of Bierman — in what has come to be known as "The Talking Play."

Minnesota had scored on an early safety but watched Northwestern take a 7-2 lead on a touchdown after a drive led by the passing of the great Otto Graham. Smith had reinjured his knee and had to be carted off the field on a stretcher. Minnesota's offense was looking hamstrung.

So when the Gophers partially blocked a punt and had the ball at the Wildcats' 41, Bierman decided it was time to unleash the trickery in a play that had been cleared with the officials.

Bob Sweiger took a handoff on a reverse and went out of bounds on the left sideline. There he jabbered with Northwestern players while the

(Above) Vic Kulbitski defends against Northwestern, in white. Gophers Wilford Garnaas (40) and Herman Frickey (33) are standing by just in case. (Bottom) An artist's rendering of the queue of fans lining up to see the champions of 1941.

Bierman, in the light trench coat, takes in the action in 1945 while players Dale Rappana (83) and Jim Shearer (54) wait to get into the game. Bierman returned as the head coach after the war but never again achieved the success he had before. He retired after the 1950 season.

referee brought the ball back into play. Meanwhile, the Minnesota linemen took their place, but all to the right of center Gene Flick, and also chatted up the Wildcats. When the ball was in place and the backfield set, and when Sweiger finally broke from his conversation, Flick quickly centered the ball sidearm to Bud Higgins, who took off down the field while the Wildcats — and the fans and the cameramen — struggled to catch up. Higgins picked up a couple of blocks by Urban Odson and scampered into the end zone. The extra point was missed, but it didn't matter, as the Gophers squeaked out an 8-7 win.

The play was the talk of the town. The following day, the *Minneapolis Star-Journal* said, "Bernie Bierman and his Golden Gophers saved their best Halloween trick for November 1 and the Northwestern Wildcats. The undefeated Gophers pulled one out of the hat in the third quarter with one of the most deceiving plays ever seen in Memorial Stadium, and certainly one of the trickiest on any American gridiron this year."

The following week brought a 9-0 win against Nebraska, and then the still-hobbled Smith begged into the lineup to lead a 34-13 victory at Iowa by having a hand in each of the team's touchdowns.

"Builder of Men"

TESTIMONIAL DINNER

FRIDAY, JANUARY 16

HOTEL MINNEAPOLIS, M

so," Coach Bernie Bierman tells Bob
Minnesota quarterback, who also has
left half and fullback by way of prov-
lity. That "just so" business isn't fool-

ing. Bierman insists on tim
all ball movements. Remem
belonged to Francis "Pug" L
Minnesota's golden 1934 era

(Above left) Interim coach George Hauser, right, has some words of advice for his players before a 1944 practice. Hauser was a teammate of Bierman's in 1915, and captain and an All-American in 1917. He went 15-11-1 filling in as coach. (Above right) Bierman instructs quarterback Bob Sandberg in the finer arts of ball handling. And that number the coach is wearing? It's the one worn by his first big star, "Pug" Lund.

The cherry on the sundae was a 41-6 bludgeoning of the Badgers at Memorial Stadium. With that, the Gophers had won their 17th game in a row and claimed an unprecedented fifth national championship in eight years, taking their place among the dynasties in sport.

MR. SMITH GOES TO HOLLYWOOD

Bruce Smith capped his glorious career by winning the Heisman Trophy, the only Heisman in Minnesota annals. A year later, before heading off to the war, Smith went to Hollywood and starred in the movie *Smith of Minnesota*

about a small-town boy who becomes an All-America halfback. It was the definition of art imitating life.

Tragically, Smith's life was cut short by cancer in August 1967 at the age of 47. But the All-America golden boy from Faribault with the movie-star good looks made his mark on countless lives. He was tireless in making the rounds to see kids at the hospital before he died, and the hospital chaplain, the Rev. William Cantwell, nominated him for sainthood in the Catholic Church.

COLLEGE FOOTBALL
ILLUSTRATED
HONOR PAGE

BERNARD W. (Bernie) BIERMAN
Head Football Coach
UNIVERSITY OF MINNESOTA

(Left) Tw...
Bo...
(Above) Bie...

Had World War II not come around to mess up the natural order of things, who knows how long Minnesota's streak would have continued? But on Pearl Harbor Day, the nation's focus changed, and so did Bierman's. He rejoined the Marine Corps and wound up coaching the Iowa Seahawks, a service team. Longtime assistant George Hauser took his place on Minnesota's sideline.

The war inspired many young men to serve, so college football teams around the country saw their ranks depleted and continuity aborted. The Gophers were no exception, although they extended their winning streak to 18 games in a 50-7 drubbing of Pitt in the first contest of the 1942 season.

The streak came to an end a week later against — in an ironic twist — the Iowa Seahawks, Bierman's new charges. The Seahawks' ranks included a number of former Gophers as well as some professional players.

the mat, and after wrestling in the 1948 Olympic games, Gagne went on to a long and illustrious pro career, launching the nationally syndicated television weekly spectacle, *All-Star Wrestling*.

BIERMAN'S BACK

Bierman returned from the service in 1945 for another run at greatness. He would find that things were different in the post-war era. The single wing had fallen out of favor to the T-formation, and his teams now had a mix of fresh-faced 18-year-olds and battle-grizzled veterans, which posed unique challenges for his disciplined style of coaching.

The Gophers opened the '45 season with four wins but then faded off the national map with five straight losses.

An influx of new talent brought a bright ray of hope in 1946. The team's newcomers would gain the nickname of the "49ers" for the run at the title they would make as seniors. Some of the names included Billy Bye, Bud Grant, Gordy Soltau, Clayton Tonnemaker and Leo Nomellini. Nomellini's first game for the Gophers happened to be the first football game in his life.

There was a three-year climb in success — 5-4 in 1946, 6-3 in 1947 and 7-2 in 1948 — building to the crescendo of 1949.

The Gophers had won their final four games in 1948, which left Minnesotans salivating. The last of those was a 16-0 victory at Wisconsin in which the battle for Paul Bunyan's Axe was born. Since 1930 the teams had been playing for the Slab of Bacon — a plaque with a letter on it reading either "M" or "W" depending on which way you held it — with the winner "bringing home the bacon." But that trophy mysteriously disappeared one year while in Wisconsin's custody, so the teams saw fit to battle for a six-foot-long axe instead. The scores of all the games in the 117-game rivalry are printed on its handle.

(Right) Halfback Dick Gregory tries to get loose against Purdue in 1949. The result was a disappointing loss for a team that had great expectations coming into the season. There was good reason for optimism, because on the team were three future Hall of Famers — Tonnemaker, Nomellini and Bud Grant — and an astounding 13 NFL draft choices among the seniors.

**10 BIG GAMES REMEMBERED:
1932-1950**

Oct. 15, 1949: Minnesota 27, Ohio State 0, in Columbus. It was the senior season for the "'49ers," a class of talented big-name players. After a 3-0 start, the Gophers hit the road and manhandled Ohio State 27-0 behind touchdowns by Billy Bye, Jim Malosky, Dick Gregory and Ken Beiersdorf to climb to No. 3. Then came a minor upset at the hands of No. 12 Michigan and a crushing loss to lowly Purdue, and the '49ers were out of the race.

THE "49ERS" FALL SHORT

The prospects of a title looked great for the '49ers, but the gold would slip through their hands. They opened with four straight convincing wins capped by a 27-0 shutout at Ohio State, which elevated them to No. 3 in the country. But the following week the team came out flat and was upset 14-7 in Ann Arbor by Michigan.

Bierman responded as he had done countless times in the past, by working his players to exhaustion the following week in practice. This time, the squad didn't respond, losing 13-7 to unranked Purdue at home. That loss cost the Gophers a shot at the Rose Bowl. Ohio State, the very team the Gophers humbled by 27 points, would earn the trip to Pasadena instead, while Minnesota finished 7-2.

Nomellini was an All-America pick for the second straight year, and he was joined by center Tonnemaker. Both would later be inducted into the College Football Hall of Fame. Nomellini went on to a brilliant 14-year career in the National Football League.

Grant, one of the great multi-sport athletes in school history, proceeded to play professional basketball for a spell and then pro football — all before embarking on a legendary coaching career and leading the Minnesota Vikings to four Super Bowls.

Bierman coached one more season in 1950, and when that campaign produced his worst record by far at 1-7-1, it was time for "The Grey Eagle" to hang up the whistle.

That season was hardly enough to tarnish what Bierman had accomplished in two decades. Out of the abyss of the Great Depression, he lifted the Gophers to unprecedented heights, and they became truly golden along the way. For the record: Five national championships in a span of eight years, with Big Ten titles in two of the intervening years and a share of the title in the year before; five undefeated seasons; a streak of 21 victories in a row and 28 games without a loss, then another streak of 18 wins; a record of 63-12-5 during the years 1932-41, with seven of those losses coming in two seasons.

Bierman ranks second in school history with a record of 93-35-6, and he was inducted into the College Football Hall of Fame in 1955. No one since then has been able to match the Bierman mystique. It would be a tall order in any era.

(Above) Bierman came a long way from the playing fields of Litchfield — All-America halfback, captain of a Big Ten champion and the coach of five national champs, a feat unrivaled in college football. (Opposite page) A Gopher locks up a tackling dummy with perfect form during a practice in 1945.

BERNIE BIERMAN
Head Football Coach
University of Minnesota
1932-41; 1945-50

National Football Foundation
and
College Hall of Fame

Coach Bernie Bierman

University of Montana 1919-1921
Mississippi State University 1925-1926
Tulane University 1927-1931
University of Minnesota 1932-1941, 1945-1950
Record 146-62-12

has been granted the highest honors of

*The National Football Foundation and College Hall of Fame,
in recognition of his outstanding coaching ability as demonstrated in intercollegiate
competition, his sportsmanship, integrity, character, and contribution to the sport of
football, this certificate bears witness that his name shall be forever honored in the
College Football Hall of Fame*

Elected 1955

NEXT: Southern comfort. A surprise from Ohio State. A star to remember. The man from Tennessee. Looking beyond the borders. Another national title. The first Rose Bowl.

1932-1950

Southern Comfort

1951-1971
Record: 97 wins, 91 losses, 11 ties

"I don't claim to be good. I knew good football players when I saw them, and I got them to come to Minnesota."

— Coach Murray Warmath

How do you fill the shoes of a legend? Sometimes it is best to recognize that those were some mighty fine shoes and move on to a new style.

That is just what the Gophers did, and the man they tabbed to replace Bernie Bierman in 1951 had some pretty good credentials himself. Forty-two-year-old Wes Fesler had spent the previous four years as the coach of Ohio State, where he had been an All-America end. He came to Minnesota with a record of 21-13-3.

In 1949, the Buckeyes had tied Michigan for the Big Ten crown and downed California 17-14 in the Rose Bowl. In 1950, they almost repeated the trick but lost to the Wolverines 9-3 in a snowstorm.

At the end of that season, Fesler announced his retirement, saying he was finished coaching. So when Minnesota athletic director Ike Armstrong announced in late January 1951 that Fesler was being signed to a three-year contract, it was a shock to most of the football world, certainly to his disbelieving fans in Ohio.

The new coach was faced with an obvious rebuilding task, and sure enough, the first year wasn't pretty. The Gophers managed to win just two games, against Nebraska and Indiana.

A STAR TO REMEMBER

However, Fesler inherited a player who could make fans forget losses and instead remember long, flashy runs. Paul Giel had grown up in Winona idolizing Bruce Smith — even insisting on playing the role of Smith in sandlot football games.

He had dreamed of being a Gopher, and now that he was here, he was feeding the dreams of Gopher fans. He played halfback, quarterback and defensive back, and also punted and returned kicks.

Giel also managed to stay busy during the spring, playing baseball under legendary coach Dick Siebert and becoming an All-America pitcher.

In a 1951 game against Purdue, Giel made perhaps the most memorable run of his career — a scrambling, serpentine spectacle that went in the books as a 64-yard touchdown but probably covered closer to 150 yards.

"I never could pick up receivers," he joked of that run. "The play was supposed to be a pass, but I couldn't see anyone so I started to run around and around. Finally, I cut back against the grain because I didn't have great speed."

(Preceding page) Fans leave Memorial Stadium after a home game in 1953. The season went well at home with a 3-1-1 record, but the Gophers only went 1-3-0 on the road. (Right) Wes Fesler came to the Gophers as head coach in 1951, just months after "retiring" at Ohio State. Fesler was a hero in Columbus, where he was a three-time consensus All-America end and an outstanding baseball and basketball player for the Buckeyes. He lasted just three years at Minnesota, posting a 10-13-4 record.

1951-1971

His speed and stats were plenty adequate. As a junior he rushed for 650 yards and threw for 643, and not only was Giel named All-American at halfback, he was selected the Big Ten MVP by the *Chicago Tribune*.

Fesler's squad was improved and finished 4-3-2, but a 21-0 loss at Michigan and ties with Purdue and Wisconsin kept it fifth in the Big Ten.

By 1953, Giel and Bob McNamara were a potent 1-2 punch in the backfield, and they helped Minnesota to some memorable wins. In late October, Michigan came to town ranked No. 5, and Fesler shocked the Wolverines by coming out in a single-wing offense. The Gophers won 22-0 to claim the Little Brown Jug for the first time since 1942. Giel worked his magic by rushing for 112 yards, throwing for 169, returning a punt 41 yards and picking off two passes.

Then the following week, having prepared for the single wing, Pittsburgh was given a steady dose of the spread offense as the Gophers stymied the Panthers 35-14. A tie in the finale against Wisconsin limited the Gophers to a 4-4-1 record.

At the end of the season, the accolades came pouring in for Giel: All-American and Big Ten MVP for the second straight year, The Associated Press Back of

10 BIG GAMES REMEMBERED:

Oct. 24, 1953
On the 50th
Little Brown
No. 5 Michiga
surprised the
Paul Giel took
169 yards, retu
two passes. It
jug since 1942

Chicag
with b
Giant:
until
Gie
1988
with Pi

(Abov
Most

career in major-league baseball rather than the National Football League.

Despite coming off a pair of decent seasons, Fesler decided at the end of his contract to "re-retire." His record was 10-13-4.

THE MAN FROM TENNESSEE

Fesler's replacement was a man from Tennessee by the name of Murray Warmath — a virtual unknown in the North. Warmath played end for the Volunteers from 1932 to 1934 and began his coaching career there as an assistant. He had been head coach at Mississippi State for two years with a record of 10-6-3.

Before Warmath was hired, there was much speculation about the new coach. The people's choice was Oklahoma's Bud Wilkinson, like Bierman a homegrown player who had starred for the Gophers. But Wilkinson and Minnesota were never were on the same page, and Armstrong decided instead on the man from the South.

So it was under this thin veil of fan disappointment — and high expectations — that Warmath took over the program. Any murmurs of discontent were squelched with some early success. The new coach was taking over a veteran team led by quarterback Gino Cappelletti and McNamara.

The Gophers went on a run to open the season, methodically downing Nebraska, Pitt, Northwestern and Illinois. By the time they headed to Michigan on Oct. 23, they had climbed to No. 8 in the AP rankings.

However, Michigan had revenge on its mind from the previous season's upset and took it to Minnesota in a big way — 34-0. But the Gophers rallied to beat Michigan State and Oregon State, setting up a home contest with Iowa.

More than 65,000 fans filled Memorial Stadium to see what turned out to be "The Bob McNamara Show." Mac scored the first Gopher touchdown, then broke a tie with an electrifying 89-yard kickoff return, which Warmath would describe as the "greatest effort of one man against 11 I have seen."

Longtime *St. Paul Pioneer Press* columnist Don Riley would later do Warmath one better, saying he watched McNamara "challenge the whole state of Iowa" on that return. He won and so did the Gophers 22-20.

McNamara overlapped just one year with his younger brother, Richard "Pinky" McNamara, a fine back in his own right who played with the Gophers

(Right) Giel grew up in Winona idolizing Heisman Trophy-winner Bruce Smith, often imitating him on the sandlots. He did a fine imitation of Smith in college as well — a triple-threat halfback/quarterback. Unlike his idol, however, Giel fell just short of a Heisman, finishing second to Notre Dame's John Lattner in the third-closest voting ever.

approached Warmath, asking if "1" would ever be called. Said the coach, "Maybe next year, when your brother has graduated."

A season-ending loss to No. 17 Wisconsin in Madison took little of the luster off a very successful debut season for Warmath.

Unexpected Success

Success was scarcer in 1955, although the Gophers still had their moments. After opening the season with three losses in four games, they returned home to face No. 1 Michigan and came within an eyelash of the big upset, falling 14-13.

The following week they turned thoughts of another upset into reality. Southern Cal came into the game ranked No. 10, but Minnesota — in a snowstorm that couldn't keep 64,000 fans away — triumphed 25-19 at The Brickhouse. There were two more losses and a 21-6 win over Wisconsin in the final game, as Warmath's sophomore season had produced a 3-6 record.

The roller-coaster Gophers turned things around in 1956. They had captain Dean Mass and All-American Bob Hobert on the offensive line, Bob "Snowshoe" Schultz, Pinky McNamara and Bob Blakely in the backfield, and a quarterback tandem of Dick Larson and Bobby Cox.

After opening the season with a 34-14 win at Washington and a 21-14 home victory over Purdue, Minnesota stalled in a scoreless tie in the rain against Northwestern. But then came another unexpected run. The Gophers downed Illinois and then headed to "The Big House" for a key contest with No. 5 Michigan.

Trailing the Wolverines 7-0, Schultz scored for the Gophers on a 30-yard run in the third quarter to cut the deficit to 7-6. Cox scored two

from 1954 to 1956 and who has been one of the university's most generous benefactors. In '54, the brothers McNamara were the two deep men on kickoff returns.

In his book *Gopher Tales*, longtime Gophers radio announcer Ray Christensen recalled that Warmath had designed reverse plays for the brothers. If "1" was called, Bob would hand the ball off to Pinky, and if "2" was called, it would be a reverse from Pinky to Bob. No. 2 worked a number of times that year, with Bob making the big gains.

One day in practice Pinky

(Above left) Michigan State's Billy Wells goes over the top of the Gophers' defense in the Spartans' 21-0 victory in 1953. The loss was no disgrace, because Michigan State went 8-1, finished No. 3 in the country and thumped unbeaten UCLA in the Rose Bowl. It was the last season as the MSU coach for Biggie Munn, the Minnesota All-America guard from the 1930s. (Left) Goldie Gopher gloats over the Little Brown Jug in '53 after the Gophers beat Michigan for the first time since 1942.

as the h

fourth-quarter touchdowns to lead Minnesota to a 20-7 win. A late field goal by Dick Borstad the following week was the key in downing Pitt 9-6, and suddenly No. 6 Minnesota was eyeing a Big Ten title.

Iowa came to town the following week and changed the picture, downing the Gophers 7-0. The Hawkeyes would clinch the title the following week while Minnesota finished its season with a 14-13 victory over Michigan State and a 13-13 tie at Wisconsin.

Minnesota finished the season 6-1-2 overall, 4-1-2 in the Big Ten, and ranked No. 9 in the UPI poll and No. 12 in the AP poll. The unexpected success put a glow on Warmath's resume, and the university's Board of Regents responded with an offer for a five-year contract extension, even though there was a year left on his original deal. He signed it and sealed his commitment to the Gophers.

Hopes were high for 1957, and the Gophers began Warmath's fourth season ranked No. 6. Early-season victories over Washington, Purdue and Northwestern elevated the ranking to No. 4 and fed the frenzy. But then, quite unexpectedly, the squad's fortunes took a turn for the worse.

It headed to Champaign as 13-point favorites against Illinois and proceeded to get toasted 34-13, scoring touchdowns late in the game after Fighting Illini coach Ray Eliot had removed some of his regulars.

10 BIG GAMES REMEMBERED: 1951-1971

Nov. 13, 1954: Minnesota 22, Iowa 20, in Minneapolis. In front of 65,000-plus fans, the Gophers beat the Hawkeyes behind Bob McNamara. "Mac" scored the first Minnesota touchdown and then, when the game was tied, put the Gophers ahead with an electrifying 89-yard kickoff return. Coach Murray Warmath described the run as the "greatest effort of one man against 11 I have seen." The winning points were scored on a safety midway through the third quarter.

(Top) A schematic drawing of the seating at Memorial Stadium in 1954. According to the drawing, capacity was just over 62,000, but 65,464 managed to cram into the stadium for the '54 game against Iowa. (Above) Cheerleaders and fans alike struggled to stay warm during a game in late 1953.

1951-1971

SM OTH ERN
CAL

UNIVERSITY OF
MINNESOTA
HOMECOMING
OCT. 29th

U of M
USC

**10 BIG GAMES REMEMBERED:
1951-1971**

Oct. 29, 1955: Minnesota 25, USC 19, in Minneapolis. A week after falling a point short against top-ranked Michigan, the Gophers shocked No. 10 USC. The game was played in snow, sleet and a 20-mph westerly wind. Bob Schultz, earning the nickname "Snowshoe," scored from 14 yards out in the first quarter, Dick Borstad rushed for 104 yards and two touchdowns, and quarterback Don Swanson had a 65-yard touchdown run.

A 24-7 home loss to Michigan would follow, along with three more defeats in the final four games, and the season that began with so much hope had taken a freefall to a 4-5 finish.

LOOKING BEYOND THE BORDERS

That gave fans cause to mumble, and Warmath a chance to explore another coaching option. He had an opportunity to return to the South and fill a vacancy at Arkansas, but in late November he announced he was content in Minnesota and committed to what he started.

However, Warmath would operate on a new platform of looking beyond Minnesota for talent. His focus turned to the East, where connections he had while an assistant at Tennessee pointed him to two talented athletes in Pennsylvania — Sandy Stephens and Judge Dickson. They would be the first in a line of African-American recruits who would achieve great success and redefine Minnesota football.

Unfortunately, the rules at the time didn't allow for freshmen to play, so their impact would have to wait. Meanwhile, the Gophers were headed for a miserable 1-8 season in 1958, the lone win coming in the next-to-last game against Michigan State. Five losses were by a touchdown or less, but the offense was anemic. And now the natives were restless.

This prompted a movement to oust Warmath as the coach, an effort that would gain momentum over time. He merely redoubled his efforts, recruiting two more blue-chip African-American athletes — Bobby Bell and Bill Munsey.

But in 1959, the losses continued to pile up. The Gophers suffered their second straight season with only one win in the Big Ten. Stephens and Dickson were in the lineup, but they failed to give instant validation to fans who had grown skeptical of Warmath's ways. Newspapermen were calling for him to step down. A group of Twin Cities businessmen upped the ante and started a campaign to raise enough money to buy out his contract. Students hanged the coach in effigy. The coach awoke one morning to find trash strewn all over his lawn.

(Preceding page) Jon Arnett, USC's All-America halfback, runs into Minnesota's All-American tackle Bob Hobert (76) as Dick McNamara (24) comes up as a reinforcement. No. 10 Southern Cal had no answers for the Gophers or the weather. A surprise snowstorm on Oct. 29, 1955, was a major factor in slowing down the high-octane Trojans. (Above right) Minnesota's Jon Jelacic (89) is blocked but plenty of other Gophers, including Dick Borstad (36), were on hand to stuff Arnett again. (Below right) Borstad rumbles through a huge hole against the Trojans. Borstad led all runners with 104 yards in the 25–19 upset in front of more than 64,000 fans who didn't let a little snow get in their way.

Warmath never once expressed any bitterness publicly. Instead, he responded with a quiet resolve — and humor. He spoke at a banquet honoring the Minneapolis high school football champs and poked fun at his plight. Said Warmath: "The test of a smart coach being run out of town on a rail is to make people think he is leading the parade."

Warmath also announced at the annual "M" Club shindig — to mixed applause — that he would be back again to coach in 1960. He had every reason to call his doubters' bluff. He had a few aces up his sleeve, and the cards were about to fall his — and the Gophers' — way.

New Talent In Town

Warmath's second wave of out-of-state recruits was now eligible to play, including Munsey and Bell.

Bell was recruited out of Shelby, North Carolina, and it helped that Warmath aide Denver Crawford knew North Carolina head coach Jim Tatum. With the South still segregated, Tatum didn't have a chance to recruit Bell, and he preferred that Bell wind up at a northern school instead of with a team on his schedule. Bell was a quarterback in high school, and fancied carrying on in that position. But Warmath, who was grooming Stephens to be his field general, was shy on talent at defensive tackle and had different ideas for the 6-foot-4, 218-pound sophomore.

The subject was broached in a meeting that Bell later recalled. "Bobby Lee," said Warmath, "you don't know it, but you're going to be one of the best tackles in the Big Ten."

"I thought he was kidding," said Bell. "Me a tackle ... why, man, we both knew I was a quarterback! So I laughed and coach, he laughed, too. But he said, 'You think it over.' So I laughed again and said 'sure' ... and forgot all about it. We started spring practice two weeks later and I was a tackle."

In addition to Bell and Munsey, the team had other new imports, including guard John Mulvena and ends Tom Hall and

(Filmstrip) A Minnesota fan runs the gamut of emotions during a 1956 game. She had plenty to cheer about — the Gophers posted their best year since the 1941 title season at 6-1-2. (Above) Murray Warmath was a bit of a surprise when he was named to succeed Fesler as coach in 1954. A former star at Tennessee, he came to Minnesota via Mississippi State. (Above right) "Smokey" Joe Salem was a fan favorite as a backup quarterback behind Sandy Stephens on the national championship team of 1960.

10 BIG GAMES REMEMBERED: 1951-1971

Nov. 5, 1960: Minnesota 27, Iowa 10, in Minneapolis. It was the clash of titans, with No. 1 Iowa taking on the No. 2 Gophers. All-American Tom Brown set the tone early by forcing a bad snap on a punt, which led to a Bill Munsey touchdown. With Iowa leading 10-7, backup quarterback Joe Salem sparked a drive resulting in a Sandy Stephens touchdown to put the Gophers on top. Scores by Roger Hagberg and Salem capped the win that lifted the Gophers to No. 1.

A happy band of Gophers cart Floyd of Rosedale off the Memorial Stadium field after they had defeated No. 1 Iowa 27-10 to take over the top spot in the polls. The reward at the end of the season would be Minnesota's first trip to the Rose Bowl.

HERE WE GO!

Rose Bowl

UNIVERSITY OF MINNESOTA 1961

SECTION 21 ROW SEAT

UNIVERSITY OF

10 BIG GAMES REMEMBERED: 1951-1971

Nov. 19, 1960: Minnesota 26, Wisconsin 7, in Madison. Minnesota kicked it into high gear late in the finale against the Badgers. After not gaining a single first down in the second and third quarters, Minnesota regained control of the game with two Sandy Stephens touchdowns in the fourth period. The victory gave the Gophers a share of the Big Ten title and a whole lot more, as the AP and UPI polls put them at No. 1, giving Minnesota its sixth national championship.

A big crowd was on hand after Minnesota ended the 1960 season with a convincing 26-7 victory over Wisconsin. The next game — the Rose Bowl — was already on the fans' minds. A few days later, it was official: The Gophers were No. 1 and headed to Pasadena to play Pacific Coast champ Washington.

Bob Deegan. Returnees included Stephens and Dickson, guard Tom Brown, tackle Frank Brixius, fullback Roger Hagberg, quarterbacks Larry Johnson and Joe Salem, and center and captain Greg Larson.

Still, no one expected much of Minnesota following three losing seasons, and an opening 26-14 win on the road against No. 12 Nebraska was treated as an anomaly. But the anomaly soon grew into a hard-to-ignore trend.

The Gophers drubbed Indiana 42-0 and shut out Northwestern 7-0, climbing to No. 10 in the rankings in the process. Two more wins followed against Illinois — with Stephens scoring all three touchdowns — and at Michigan. The doubters were becoming believers. After Minnesota crushed Kansas State 48-7 in a non-conference game, the stage was set for a showdown — the No. 2 Gophers against No. 1 Iowa.

Earlier in the week, Tom Brown had roused the fans during a pep rally, predicting a win for the Gophers, and he did his best to terrorize the Hawkeyes

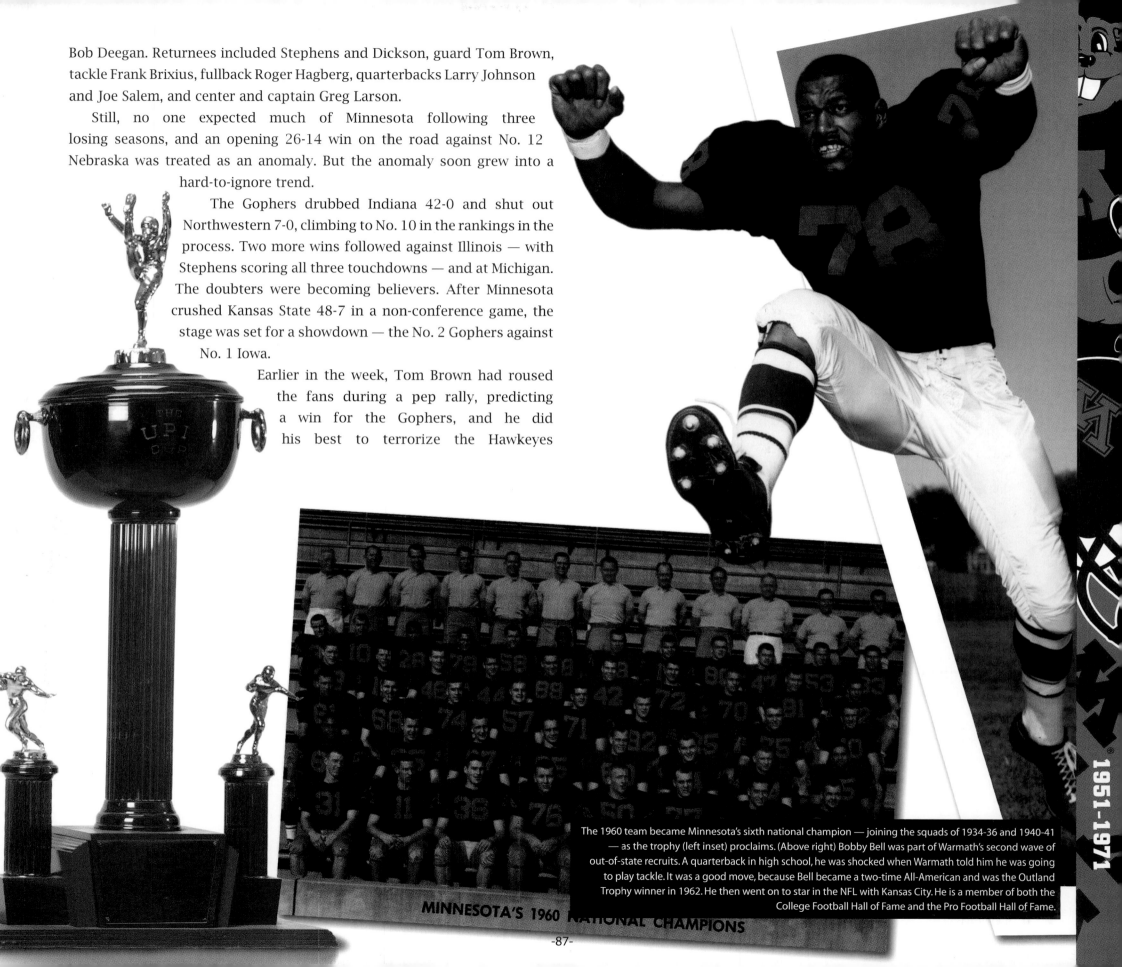

The 1960 team became Minnesota's sixth national champion — joining the squads of 1934-36 and 1940-41 — as the trophy (left inset) proclaims. (Above right) Bobby Bell was part of Warmath's second wave of out-of-state recruits. A quarterback in high school, he was shocked when Warmath told him he was going to play tackle. It was a good move, because Bell became a two-time All-American and was the Outland Trophy winner in 1962. He then went on to star in the NFL with Kansas City. He is a member of both the College Football Hall of Fame and the Pro Football Hall of Fame.

MINNESOTA'S 1960 NATIONAL CHAMPIONS

**10 BIG GAMES REMEMBERED:
1951-1971**

Oct. 28, 1961: Minnesota 23, Michigan 20, in Minneapolis. Two days before the game, Gopher quarterback Sandy Stephens got married. The new bridegroom fumbled twice early in the game, leading to two Michigan touchdowns, but then he sparked a big comeback. First he broke free for a 63-yard touchdown run, then later connected with Jack Campbell on a 46-yard touchdown pass. A Judge Dickson TD run finished off the comeback.

DEN THE WOLVERINES
OCT. 28 1961
U. of MINN.
HOMECOMING

HOMECOMING

MINNESOTA
MICHIGAN

GOPHER GOALPOST
OFFICIAL PROGRAM 35c

would be the first Rose Bowl appearance ever for Minnesota.

The team soaked up the experience, basking in luxury at the Huntington Hotel and accepting kudos for its fine season. The game itself would prove to be another matter.

Washington came out firing on all cylinders and built a 17-0 halftime lead while Minnesota's offense sputtered. The second half

The Gophers celebrate another win over Michigan and another capture of the Little Brown Jug. Minnesota beat the Wolverines four straight times from 1960 to 1963. It is the second-longest winning streak over Michigan ever. The "golden-era" teams won nine in a row from 1934 to 1942.

was a different story, with Minnesota piling up 12 first downs to the Huskies' one and pulling within 17-7 when Stephens pitched to Munsey for a touchdown.

That's the way the game ended, but it did nothing to tarnish a brilliant rags-to-riches story.

Brown, who had been as mean-spirited to his other opponents as he was to Iowa, reaped the rewards. He was named consensus All-American, Big Ten MVP and won the Outland Trophy, given to the nation's best interior lineman. He also finished second in balloting for the Heisman Trophy.

Warmath received the ultimate vindication, being named national Coach of the Year. One year after he had been hung in effigy, fans were sporting buttons saying, "Murray Warmath for President."

The commander-in-chief of the Gophers had his work cut out for him in 1961. The team graduated 13 seniors, including stalwarts Brown, Larson, Hagberg, Brixius and Salem.

But there was plenty of returning talent, and one particularly promising sophomore from Winston-Salem, North Carolina — Carl Eller. Eller was a 6-foot-5, 240-pound specimen and found himself being compared to, and on the same line with, Bobby Lee Bell. Enough said.

The opening opponent was Missouri, which the Gophers had supplanted at the top of the ratings the previous year. Mizzou got its revenge, prevailing 6-0 in the rain, snow and wind.

A Mental Honeymoon

Minnesota then squeaked by Oregon 14-7 to start another impressive streak. Road wins followed against Northwestern and Illinois. Then came a pair of home victories against Michigan and Michigan State.

The Michigan game provided some interesting drama, centered around Stephens. Two days earlier, he had gotten married — not your typical midseason football occurrence — and it looked early on as if Stephens was on a mental honeymoon. He fumbled twice, leading to two Michigan touchdowns.

Then Stephens took over the game, first breaking loose for a 63-yard touchdown run. After the Wolverines extended their lead to 20-8 heading into the fourth quarter, Stephens hit Jack Campbell with a 46-yard touchdown strike, and Dickson finished off the comeback with a touchdown run

MINNESOTA
VERSUS
UCLA

Official Program
JANUARY 1, 1962

Rose Bowl
PASADENA, CALIF.

50¢

OFFICIAL
UNIVERSITY OF MINNESOTA
1961
ROSE BOWL TOUR
●
SPONSORED BY:
THE MINNESOTA ALUMNI ASSOCIATION
310 Coffman Memorial Union
Minneapolis 14, Minnesota

1951-1971

"Goldie" Gopher Returns To

PASADENA

ROSE BOWL
61-62

UNIVERSITY OF MINNESOTA FOOTBALL FACT BOOK

Bowl Edition

to make it 22-20. Stephens finished with a combined 304 yards rushing and passing.

After victories against Iowa and Purdue, the third-ranked Golden Gophers needed just one more win against Wisconsin to claim their second straight Big Ten title. But the Badgers had other ideas, and their 23-21 upset victory dropped Minnesota to second place.

Ohio State was the Big Ten champion, but the Buckeyes declined the offer to play in the Rose Bowl, so the Gophers were invited instead.

The second time around, Warmath eschewed the fancy hotel in favor of a monastery, and his players responded with a quiet resolve. After UCLA tallied an early field goal, it was all Gophers. Dickson recovered a fumble on the Bruins' 6-yard line, and three plays later Stephens scored from a yard out. He then orchestrated a 75-yard drive before halftime, with Munsey doing the honors on a 3-yard reverse off left tackle. The final drive was an 11-minute, 84-yard beauty capped by a 2-yard Stephens jaunt. Final score: Minnesota 21, UCLA 3. The Gophers had stymied the Bruins' single wing, and Stephens was named the outstanding player.

Stephens finished the season with 1,151 yards in total offense and, like Brown the year before, was named the Big Ten MVP. Bell and Stephens were named All-Americans, with Stephens becoming the first African-American to claim that honor at quarterback.

ON THE DEFENSIVE

Many of the big names were gone in '62 — Stephens, Dickson, Mulvena and Hall from the offense — but there was plenty of defense left to go around, especially the two-headed monster of Bell and Eller on the line.

The Gophers responded with a record-breaking defensive showing, allowing only 58.2 yards rushing per game in conference

(Above left) Warmath gets a victory ride following the 1962 Rose Bowl victory over UCLA. After his team stayed in a posh hotel the year before in Pasadena, he put them in a monastery to prepare for the '62 game against the Bruins. (Opposite page) Judge Dickson (25), who made a key fumble recovery earlier, churns for some tough yards against UCLA. Dickson earned his law degree from Minnesota and later became — what else? — a judge.

INTERCOLLEGIATE FOOTBALL
NEW YEAR'S DAY, 1962 — 2 P.M.

TUNNEL
16

ROW
39

SEAT
16

ENTER GATE F

PASADENA
ROSE BOWL

Est. Price $5.55
Fed. Tax .45
TOTAL $6.00

**10 BIG GAMES REMEMBERED:
1951-1971**

Jan. 1, 1962: Minnesota 21, UCLA 3, in Pasadena. The smell of roses was much sweeter for the Gophers the second time around. After UCLA jumped out to an early 3-0 lead, Judge Dickson recovered a fumble deep in UCLA territory, and Minnesota converted three plays later on a 1-yard Sandy Stephens run. The lead was extended when Bill Munsey capped a 75-yard drive with a 3-yard touchdown run before halftime. Stephens was named the game's outstanding player.

1951-1971

play. Throw away a 34-22 loss to Northwestern in the third week of the season, and Minnesota only surrendered 13 points to seven other opponents heading into the Wisconsin game.

That put the Big Ten title on the line in the finale against the Badgers. The Gophers came into the game ranked No. 5 while the Badgers were No. 3, and as everyone expected, it came down to the wire.

Minnesota led 6-0 on quarterback Duane Blaska's 15-yard pass to Jim Cairns, and again 9-7 on Collin Versich's 32-yard field goal. But late in the game the Badgers drove downfield behind the passing of quarterback Ron VanderKelen. At the Minnesota 43, VanderKelen dropped back to pass and was hit by Bell, with the ball floating into the arms of the Gophers' John Perkovich for an apparent interception. But a roughing penalty was called on Bell, and Wisconsin had the ball back, plus 15 yards. Warmath lost his cool and got flagged for another 15 yards for unsportsmanlike conduct. The Badgers punched the ball in to take a 14-9 lead.

The Gophers had one final drive — aided by three penalties on the Badgers — but on first down at the Wisconsin 14, Blaska was picked off in the end zone. The Badgers had stolen Minnesota's thunder.

Warmath later expressed deep disappointment in taking that penalty. He was pardoned, though, in a manner of speaking. In his book, Christensen recounted a tale from the following week. Bell was honored at halftime of the Army-Navy game and got to shake hands with President John F. Kennedy. Said Kennedy, "I thought you really got robbed in the Wisconsin game."

All that was left was the annual Minnesota hardware collection, and this time it was Bell's turn to shine. For the second straight year he was named All-American at tackle, and became the second Gopher in three years to win the Outland Trophy. He finished third in the Heisman voting.

Maybe it was good that Warmath got Bell used to switching positions. In the NFL, Kansas City moved Bell to linebacker, where he became an All-Pro for eight straight seasons and helped the Chiefs to two Super

10 BIG GAMES REMEMBERED: 1951-1971

Nov. 25, 1967: Minnesota 21, Wisconsin 14, in Minneapolis. Minnesota entered the final game of the season with a 5-1 conference record and needing a victory — coupled with a Purdue win over Indiana — to go to the Rose Bowl. The Gophers responded with a 21-14 victory over the Badgers to finish in a three-way tie for the Big Ten title, but the Hoosiers beat Purdue to earn a trip to Pasadena. That 1967 group of Gophers is the last to win a Big Ten championship.

(Above left) Minnesota players had some anxious moments on the bench during the 1967 Wisconsin game. The Gophers won 21-14 and earned a share of the Big Ten title, but Indiana received the bid to the Rose Bowl. (Left) Cheerleaders lead the way onto the field through the snow before the game against the Badgers.

Bowls. He joined teammate Tom Brown in the College Football Hall of Fame, and in 1983 he was inducted into the Pro Football Hall of Fame.

One More Joyride

The ensuing four years were up and down. Warmath posted records of 3-6 in 1963, 5-4 in 1964, 5-4-1 in 1965 and 4-5-1 in 1966. But there were a couple of bright spots: A tie with No. 7 USC in the '65 opener and an upset of Ohio State in '66.

Eller, who would go on to a Pro Football Hall of Fame career as a member of the Minnesota Vikings' "Purple People Eaters," was named All-American in 1963, and end Aaron Brown earned the same honor in 1965.

There would be one more joyride for Warmath in 1967. Similar to 1962, everything was decided on the final week of the season against Wisconsin. The Gophers were 5-1 in the Big Ten, and in the last two weeks had whipped Indiana 33-7 and lost 41-12 at Purdue. That set up a strange situation: If Purdue were to beat Indiana in the final game, it would be the Big Ten champion but unable to go to the Rose Bowl under terms of a new Big Ten-Pacific Coast contract that said a team couldn't go to Pasadena two years in a row. That would open the door for Minnesota.

While the Gophers were taking care of business against the Badgers 21-14, Indiana toppled Purdue to create a three-way tie with the Gophers and Boilermakers for the title. Since the Hoosiers had never gone to Pasadena, they received the invitation.

But the share of the championship was noteworthy. It marked the last time the Gophers have had even a piece of the Big Ten title — a streak that has now exceeded four decades. Members of that team, which included Pro Football Hall of Fame tight end Charlie Sanders, were honored at halftime of a 2007 game for their accomplishment.

There would be one more winning season for Warmath in 1968 on a team led by two-time All-American end Bob Stein. Three subsequent subpar seasons would mark the end for the man from Tennessee.

Warmath's 1971 Gophers saw fit to send him off in style. In the season finale against — who else? — Wisconsin, the Gophers trailed late in the game but came up with one last drive in the closing seconds, and when quarterback Craig Curry hit Mel Anderson with a 12-yard pass in the corner of the end zone, Warmath had gained his 87th victory in 18 seasons.

(Right) Jim Carter (34) goes up and over some Wolverines in 1967 when Minnesota again took home the Little Brown Jug with a 20-15 victory. Carter played a lot of fullback for the Gophers but made his mark in the NFL as a linebacker for the Green Bay Packers for nine years.

NO ANSWER IN NUMBERS

Warmath's final record was 87-78-7, but his contributions to Gopher football can't be explained in numbers.

He brought forth the novel notion that, to keep up with the Joneses, Minnesota needed to actively seek out the Stephenses — and the Bells and the Ellers.

He stuck to his guns and with Minnesota, even through the times when Minnesota wasn't sure it wanted to stick with him.

He survived with his humor intact, and an undying devotion to Minnesota.

I spoke with the 95-year-old Warmath in late March 2008, and his humor still shines through. "I don't feel like I'm over 60 at all; I feel like I'm 40," he said. He appreciates his coaching career and allowed that he wouldn't mind still being in the game, but "it doesn't look like anyone's looking for a coach that old."

He still beams about players like Stephens and McNamara and Bell, and downplays his own role in all the success. "I don't claim to be good," he said. "I knew good football players when I saw them, and I got them to come to Minnesota. I've enjoyed every bit of it."

At his most recent birthday celebration, Minnesota announced that the home locker room in the new on-campus football stadium will be named in his honor.

That locker room will be filled with some of the best players available to Minnesota at the time, not just from the Land of 10,000 Lakes, but from all around the country.

Warmath would have it no other way.

> ### 10 BIG GAMES REMEMBERED: 1951-1971
>
> **Nov. 20, 1971:** Minnesota 23, Wisconsin 21, in Minneapolis. After 18 years at the helm of the Golden Gophers, this would be Murray Warmath's last game, and his players saw to it that his tenure ended in style. Needing a touchdown to win, Minnesota took the ball at its 20 with 2:08 remaining. One glorious 80-yard drive later, Craig Curry floated a 12-yard touchdown pass to Mel Anderson with nine seconds remaining, and Warmath and the Gophers had the win.

(Left) Warmath wasn't the people's choice in 1954 — Oklahoma coach and Minnesota alum Bud Wilkinson was — but he won them over in 18 years as the Gophers' head coach. He is the only Minnesota coach other than Bernie Bierman to win a national championship, and only Henry "Doc" Williams coached more years. (Opposite page) A full house in Memorial Stadium is ready for some action before a game with Wisconsin in the 1970s. The Gophers left their on-campus home after the 1981 season but will return home in 2009 to play in a new stadium.

NEXT: On the outside looking in. A quiet leader. The magical season. A real workhorse. Another "M" man. "The Hurlin' Hawaiian." Nightmare on Chicago Avenue.

1951-1971

ON THE OUTSIDE LOOKING IN

1972-1983
RECORD: 58 WINS, 74 LOSSES, 1 TIE

"Stoll's teams won half their games and they won some games they had no business winning — mainly, that jewel against Michigan last year … It made folks expect too much."

— A local broadcaster on the firing of coach Cal Stoll

When Murray Warmath left Minnesota, the time seemed right for another "M" man to return to lead the Golden Gophers, and Cal Stoll was chosen for the task.

Stoll was a high school fullback for his six-man team in Valley City, North Dakota, about an hour west of the Minnesota border. After a long stint in the Navy, Stoll played in 1948 and '49 for Bernie Bierman. He could have played another season had he not accelerated his studies to graduate early in 1950.

His last coaching stop before Minnesota was at Wake Forest. He led the Demon Deacons to consecutive winning seasons for the first time in almost 20 years and the Atlantic Coast Conference title in 1970.

Stoll was taking over the Gophers during the heyday of the "Big Two, Little Eight" era, and anyone who followed Big Ten football in the 1970s and '80s knows exactly what that was and, to some extent, still is. Each year, the conference race would be decided between two teams — Ohio State and Michigan — and everyone else was left to fight for the crumbs.

But Stoll would fare better than most, thanks to a parade of talented skill-position players, a number of whom would etch their names in the record book.

The 1972 season opener offered a glimpse at his team's talents, although the result was a 27-23 loss at Indiana. Running back John King rushed for 174 yards and Bob Morgan added 127 more.

Four more losses would follow before Stoll notched his first win — a decisive 43-14 whipping of Iowa in which King gained 173 yards. But the season would end on a high note with three wins in a row against Northwestern, Michigan State and Wisconsin, giving Stoll an opening campaign of 4-7.

The workhorse King set a single-season rushing record with 1,164 yards and 11 touchdowns on 237 carries.

King was joined in the backfield the following year by two talented and explosive players, Rick Upchurch and Larry Powell. Upchurch had breakaway speed and was an outstanding special teams performer, returning both punts and kickoffs. Those all-purpose skills later served Upchurch well in his professional career with the Denver Broncos.

(Preceding page) Strike up the band! The Minnesota marching band struts past the fraternity houses before the 1977 homecoming game against Northwestern. The inspiration helped, as the Gophers beat the Wildcats 13-7. (Right) Cal Stoll was an "M" man, the kind the school wanted to replace Murray Warmath in 1972. He was a former player under Bernie Bierman in the late 1940s, and he had worked some magic at Wake Forest by winning the Atlantic Coast Conference title in 1970 — the Demon Deacons' first ACC crown ever.

1972-1983

Powell's saga was short and bittersweet. Recruited by Stoll out of Michigan, Powell would play just one year for the Gophers. In the offseason he came down with Guillain-Barré Syndrome, an affliction that almost cost him his life. Powell withered to 115 pounds before making a recovery. He was not able to return to football.

A Quiet Leader

Yet another Stoll recruit who arrived on the scene in '73 was Tony Dungy, a svelte quarterback from Jackson, Michigan. He came to Minnesota to play both football for Stoll and basketball for Bill Musselman. But Dungy decided to hang up the sneakers after his freshman year and concentrate on football.

All that talent made for a good season for the Gophers in 1973. They finished with a four-game winning streak and a 7-4 record for third place in the Big Ten, and three of the four losses came against teams ranked No. 4 or higher in The Associated Press poll — Ohio State, Nebraska and Michigan.

In late-season wins against Northwestern, Purdue and Wisconsin, Upchurch ran for 154, 177 and 167 yards, respectively. For his career, Upchurch averaged more than 6 yards per carry, still a team record.

Dungy ran the offense from 1974-76, three moderately successful seasons of 4-7, 6-5 and 6-5. He finished his career near the top of almost every school passing category, including yards (3,515) and total offense (4,680), and was also a two-time Academic All-Big Ten pick.

Dungy wasn't flashy, but he was a soft-spoken, effective leader and a student of the game. Those same traits still define the man who has gone on to great success in the National Football League.

Dungy was a safety for the Pittsburgh Steelers for two years and played in the Super Bowl XIII win over the Dallas Cowboys. Then it was onto coaching, first with the Gophers as a defensive backs coach, then as an assistant in the NFL with the Steelers, Chiefs and Vikings.

His first head coaching stint with the Tampa Bay Buccaneers was a success, and he has been even more prolific at Indianapolis, overseeing a powerhouse that won the Super Bowl in 2007, making Dungy the first black head coach to win a Super Bowl title. Uniformly described as humble and gracious, Dungy is class personified.

A Magical Season

The 1977 season was magical for the Gophers, despite what would be only a fifth-place finish in the conference. They had a solid defense, led by a trio of linebackers — Steve Stewart, Mark Merrill and Mike Hunt — who would all go on to be second-round NFL draft choices. And there

Coach Stoll talks with one of his players before the '72 season, in which the Gophers would go 4-7 but finish with a three-game winning streak. Notice on the wall behind Stoll the photo (center, bottom row) of one of the most famous alumni of his former employer, Wake Forest — golfing legend Arnold Palmer.

were a variety of weapons on offense, including wide receiver Jeff Anhorn, fullback Kent Kitzmann and a true freshman running back from Michigan, Marion Barber Jr.

After a season-opening win against Western Michigan, the Gophers fell 38-7 to Ohio State, with the only points coming on a 100-yard kickoff return by Bobby Weber. Then came two games against Pac 8 opponents that would showcase what the team could do.

First, they dominated No. 18 UCLA 27-13. Bruins coach Terry Donahue had given the Gophers some bulletin board material when he said Minnesota wouldn't be the most talented team his team would face that year. The "talent-challenged" defense was all over the field, recovering six fumbles and intercepting two passes, and by the time the lead grew to 27-7, UCLA had a measly five first downs and 99 net yards.

The next week produced another victory against Washington, and in a span of two weeks, the Gophers had upset the two teams that would fight that season for a bid to the Rose Bowl.

After a road loss to Iowa, the Gophers rebounded with a win against Northwestern, and then Michigan came to town. The biggest game of the Stoll era was played on Oct. 22, 1977.

The largest home crowd of the season turned out to watch the Golden Gophers take on the No. 1 Wolverines. A wise man wouldn't have bet a hot dog against a year's worth of steak dinners on the Gophers. The Wolverines had just throttled Wisconsin 56-0 and earlier in the season routed No. 5 Texas A&M 41-3. Further, they hadn't been shut out in 112 games, a streak dating back to 1967 — the same year the Gophers were last able to pry the Little Brown Jug out of the Wolverines' hands.

CALLING ON AN OLD HAND

On Friday morning, Stoll asked longtime Gophers assistant coach George "Butch" Nash to speak to the players after the evening dinner at the Leamington Hotel.

The honest and earnest Nash, who was on the jug-winning teams of 1936, '37 and '38 in the Bierman years, poured his heart out to his rapt audience. He talked about Sig Harris and the famous game of 1903, and his own team in the mid-1930s on which Harris was a coach; about the privilege of playing football and the obligation of playing for your teammates; about what it means to hear The Rouser and go out and do battle for the University of Minnesota ... and for yourself.

For five minutes Nash talked, and when he finished, many of the players were in tears.

The Gophers carried that emotion into the game and came out fearless and firing. On the second play of the first drive, sophomore Mark Carlson, who was making his first start, hit Anhorn with a 23-yard pass to set the tone, and Minnesota marched to a Paul Rogind field goal.

When Michigan got the ball back, Merrill immediately unloaded on star quarterback Rick Leach as he was pitching the ball, and Keith Brown recovered at the Wolverines' 12-yard line. "I was assigned the quarterback," Merrill said. "I tried to hit him as hard as I could, and I really don't think he was quite the same for the rest of the game."

On a fourth-down play a moment later, Barber scored from 3 yards out.

Minnesota would tack on two more field goals by Rogind, who was from Michigan, and the team had an emotional, watershed 16-0 victory. Michigan could muster only four first downs rushing and 202 total yards.

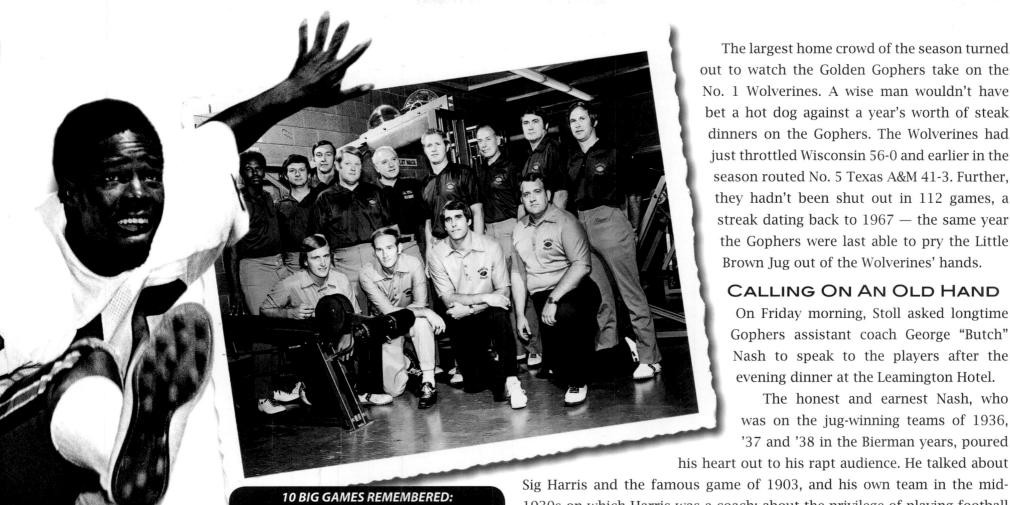

10 BIG GAMES REMEMBERED: 1972-1983

Nov. 24, 1973: Minnesota 19, Wisconsin 17, in Minneapolis. Minnesota finished coach Cal Stoll's second season with a four-game winning streak, capped by a win over Wisconsin at Memorial Stadium. Rick Upchurch had 14 carries for 167 yards and two touchdowns, John King had 86 yards and Larry Powell ran for the final touchdown. The Gophers wound up with a 7-4 record and a 6-2 mark in the Big Ten, good for sole possession of third place.

(Above) Stoll — fifth from left in the back row — with his 1974 coaching staff. (Inset) Rick Upchurch was one of Stoll's first prized recruits, a multi-talented player who could run, catch and return kicks. Upchurch went on to have a stellar nine-year career in the NFL with the Denver Broncos as a receiver and kick returner.

1972-1983

Gary Acromite (66) and an official signal touchdown as Jeff Thompson plows in for one of his two scores against UCLA in 1977. The victory was one of two straight — Washington was the other a week later— over Pac-8 teams that would fight for that league's title and a Rose Bowl berth.

10 BIG GAMES REMEMBERED: 1972-1983

Sept. 24, 1977: Minnesota 27, UCLA 13, in Minneapolis. UCLA came into Memorial Stadium ranked No. 18 and a solid favorite to beat Minnesota. Instead, the Gophers dominated from start to finish, getting two touchdown runs by Jeff Thompson, a fumble return for a touchdown by Steve Midboe and two Paul Rogind field goals. By the time the Gophers were up 27-7, they had held the Bruins to only five first downs and 99 net yards.

The Gophers gave a game ball to Nash, and the man who explained the value of "The Jug" did the honors of carrying it into the locker room.

"It's the greatest victory I have ever experienced," Stoll said after the game. He was not alone in that sentiment.

The Golden Gophers jumped into the national rankings at No. 19 in the AP poll, their first appearance there since 1969, and the only one in Stoll's years.

As high as the Gophers were flying, there was bound to be a letdown, but the altimeter reading bottomed out the next week. They lost 34-22 on the road to Indiana and followed that up with their only home loss of the season, 29-10 to Michigan State.

A Real Workhorse

However, Stoll was able to rally the team the final two weeks of the season, and Minnesota closed with a 21-0 victory at Illinois and a 13-7 win over Wisconsin at home.

One player did more than his share in those two games. Kitzmann, a sophomore from Rochester, came into the Illinois game with 54 carries and 227 yards for the season. Against the Fighting Illini, he toted the ball 57 times for 266 yards, breaking a number of NCAA, Big Ten and team records in the process. It was Kitzmann left, Kitzmann right, Kitzmann up the middle. Rinse and repeat.

At one point he had 13 consecutive carries. If Illinois ever figured out that Kitzmann would be getting the ball on virtually every play, it did nothing to stonewall him. His longest gain was 22 yards, and he never once lost yardage.

Kitzmann was the plow horse again in the Wisconsin game, rushing another 40 times for 154 yards. Yes, 97 carries in back-to-back games was also an NCAA record.

That earned the Gophers an invitation to the inaugural Hall of Fame Classic in Birmingham, Alabama, on Dec. 22 — their first appearance in a bowl game since the '62 Rose Bowl.

Playing Maryland on a chilly evening, the Gophers came out hot. Led by quarterback Wendell Avery, they marched 66 yards in 11 plays, capped by a 1-yard run by Barber. Their second drive started promisingly, but Barber's fumble deep in Terp territory brought an abrupt end to the momentum. Maryland scored all 17 of its points in the remainder of the first half. The Gophers finished on the southern end of a 17-7 score.

It was Barber's turn to be great in '78. The sophomore had 100 yards or more rushing in each of the Gophers' five victories. In a midseason 22-20 defeat of Iowa, he ran for 130. Three weeks later, he rushed for 177 yards and scored three touchdowns in a thrilling 32-31 victory against Indiana. Minnesota trailed 24-7 at halftime — despite having gained 320 yards — and fell behind 31-14 in the fourth quarter before Avery

(Above left) The Gophers, along with Goldy, charge onto the field before the 1977 Michigan game. (Above) After the Michigan game, linebacker Steve Stewart hoists the Little Brown Jug, the first time a Minnesota player had been able to do that in a decade. (Right) Quarterback Mark Carlson (12) congratulates Marion Barber (41) after his touchdown run against the Wolverines sealed the 16-0 victory.

10 BIG GAMES REMEMBERED: 1972-1983

Oct. 22, 1977: Minnesota 16, Michigan 0, in Minneapolis. Michigan came in ranked No. 1 and hadn't been shut out in 112 games, which made the Gophers' upset one of the greatest games in Minnesota history. The Gopher defense dominated, picking off Rick Leach twice, recovering three fumbles and holding Michigan to four first downs rushing. Marion Barber's 3-yard touchdown run and Paul Rogind's three field goals were more than enough offense.

1972-1983

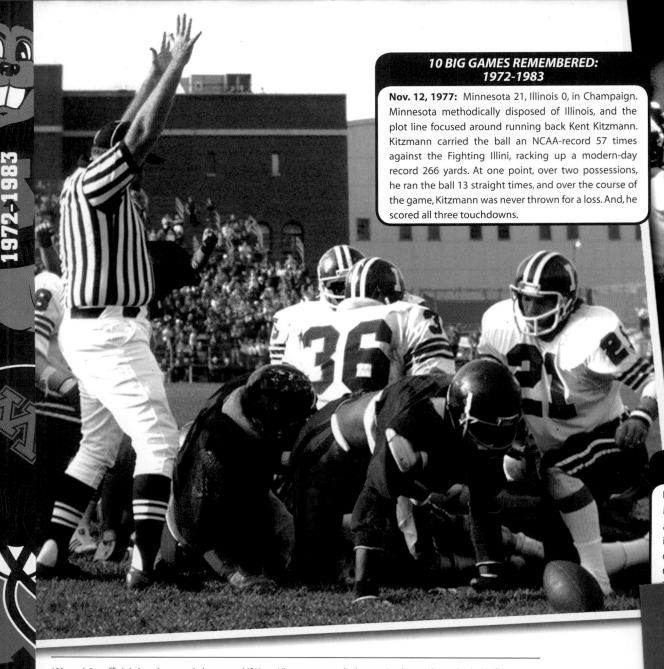

(Above) An official signals a touchdown, and if Kent Kitzman was a little too tired to pick up the ball after one of his three TDs against Illinois in 1977, he could be excused. Kitzman carried the ball an NCAA-record 57 times against the Fighting Illini, including 13 in a row over one stretch. (Above right) A Maryland runner finds some daylight against the Gophers in the Hall of Fame Bowl in '77. The Gophers lost, but the season was still a triumph, because the bowl appearance was Minnesota's first in 15 years and only the third ever.

and Barber engineered a remarkable comeback. Rogind nailed a 31-yard field goal with five seconds left for the win. The Gophers set modern-era records for offensive plays (109) and total yards (577).

Against Illinois two weeks later, Barber ran for a career-high 233 yards in a 24-6 win. He finished the season with 1,210 yards rushing, eclipsing the record set by King six years earlier.

The win against Illinois would prove to be Stoll's last. A 48-10 drubbing by Wisconsin left Minnesota with its second straight 4-4 mark in the Big Ten, but

without the sa
of his duties b
ANOTHER
Stoll's seven-y
teams able to
away the 1-13
were 26-16 aga

As one loc
games and they
that jewel again
It made folks ex

(Below) Wendell Avery celebrates after a score against Indiana. Despite setting a batch of team offensive records, the Gophers had to come off the deck with 18 fourth-quarter points to win. (Inset) Stoll was let go after seven seasons and a 39-39 record by athletic director Paul Giel. Apathy among the fans was one of the reasons. In his last year, only the Iowa game drew more than 50,000 fans, and most of the time, the stadium was half-full.

el fires Stoll; new
otball coach may be
amed within month

10 BIG GAMES REMEMBERED: 1972-1983

Nov. 4, 1978: Minnesota 32, Indiana 31, in Minneapolis. It took a furious comeback for the Gophers to pull out a 32-31 victory in a game they thoroughly dominated, setting team records for offensive plays (109) and total yards (577). The Achilles heel was six fumbles. Quarterback Wendell Avery and running back Marion Barber led the charge after the Gophers trailed the Hoosiers 31-14 in the fourth quarter. Paul Rogind kicked the game-winning 31-yard field goal with five seconds left.

1972-1983

NIGHTMARE ON CHICAGO AVENUE

But just as things began to take on a rosy hue, everything turned to black. That three-game winning streak was followed by eight consecutive losses, and of those eight, only two were by 10 points or fewer.

Things would get even worse for Salem and the Gophers in 1983. There was an opening-game victory at Rice, snapping the eight-game skid. But then Tom Osborne's high-flying No. 1-ranked Nebraska Cornhuskers came to town.

The Huskers featured an array of speedy backs and receivers, including Turner Gill, Mike Rozier, Irving Fryar and Jeff Smith, and they decided to turn the Dome's artificial turf into their own private racetrack. Nebraska won 84-13, as it rushed for 585 yards on 52 carries and finished with 780 total yards of offense. The Huskers scored three touchdowns in every quarter, and their 12 scoring drives took a total of 13:41 in elapsed time.

After the game, Osborne apologized and swore he wasn't trying to run up the score. "It just seemed like every time I was looking up, we were scoring."

The "Nightmare on Chicago Avenue" took a dubious place in Gopher annals: It was the most points ever given up and the most lopsided defeat, surpassing a 56-7 loss to Ohio State in 1973 and a 54-0 shutout at the hands of Nebraska in 1974 — the last time they played.

There would be more carnage that year. Two weeks later, the Buckeyes handed the Gophers a 69-18 defeat in Columbus, and a couple of weeks after that, Wisconsin came to town and won 56-17. A second straight defeat to Northwestern the following week made it six losses in a row and would serve as the last straw.

Salem resigned effective the end of the season, and the Gophers limped to the finish with a 1-10 record, surrendering 518 points for the season.

Maybe the ghosts of Memorial Stadium were unhappy the team moved away. Or maybe this had just been a character-builder for fans, so that they would be able to appreciate a good turnaround. They would soon get their wish.

10 BIG GAMES REMEMBERED: 1972-1983

Sept. 17, 1983: Nebraska 84, Minnesota 13, in Minneapolis. No. 1-ranked Nebraska came into the Metrodome and ran up the score in record-breaking fashion. The Cornhuskers scored three touchdowns in each quarter, rushed for 585 yards and amassed 780 yards in total offense. It was the most lopsided defeat in history, and Nebraska's 84 points were the most given up. Two weeks later, Minnesota lost 69-18 to Ohio State on the way to surrendering 518 points for the season.

(Left) A cartoon celebrated 100 years of Minnesota football in 1982. The first team in 1882 went 1-1, while the team a century later went 3-8. (Opposite page) Salem just couldn't get the Gophers smokin' again. After seven years and a 19-35-1 record, he was let go in 1983.

the noose being eadied for Salem?

1972-1983

NEXT: Sweet Lou. A downturn Downtown. Forecast is Foggie. Bittersweet Lou. A homegrown star. The sound of silence. Struggling to find success.

A Downtown Downturn

"Over 100,000 Michigan fans sat in stunned silence, the most thrilling lack of sound I can ever remember."

— Announcer Ray Christensen on the 1986 upset of Michigan

A month after the 1983 season ended, Minnesota announced that its new head coach would be a well-known figure by the name of Lou Holtz.

Holtz's college coaching credentials were without question. He had spent the last seven seasons at Arkansas guiding the Razorbacks to six bowl appearances and a record of 60-21-2, the best winning percentage in team history. In his first season there, Arkansas went 11-1, upset Oklahoma in the Orange Bowl and Holtz was named Coach of the Year.

The Razorbacks and their animated coach had become a staple on national TV, and Minnesota was more than happy to lure him northward.

"Sweet Lou" was an idea man, brimming with confidence at the prospects of resurrecting a football program that had languished since the mid-1960s. He could talk a mile a minute, and sometimes his words were left struggling to keep up with his thoughts. And he was blessed with a sense of humor to get him through what promised to be a rocky beginning.

After all, this was a team that had lost 18 of its last 19 — including 17 straight in the Big Ten — and had given up an NCAA-record 518 points the previous season.

"That's almost more than our basketball team gave up," Holtz joked on one occasion. Another time he said of his situation, "There's more here than I can say grace over."

Those flashes of humor were a big part of the charm that made him an instant idol of fans, and his one-liners were worthy of a highlight reel. An article in *Mpls-St.Paul* magazine, aptly titled "A new spiritual folk hero," compiled a sampling of Holtzisms. On his claim to fill the Metrodome with season-ticket holders in two years: "If we don't sell 62,500 season tickets in 1986, we're moving the team to Tampa." On recruiting the Minnesota athlete: "The body and soul of this football program must come from Minnesota. Of course, the arms and legs will have to come from somewhere else."

THE "FOGGIE-EST" IDEA

The arms and the legs of one player wound up being a big boost for Holtz. Rickey Foggie came to Minnesota from Waterloo, South Carolina, and he soon became the flashiest quarterback ever to wear the maroon and gold, destined to set a number of school records. Foggie was an adept passer, and he ran the option like no other quarterback has in these parts.

(Preceding page) Minnesota's move to the Hubert H. Humphrey Metrodome in downtown Minneapolis from the campus wasn't well received by many of the Gophers' faithful. Games will be moved back to campus in 2009 in a new stadium. (Right) Lou Holtz was a wildly popular — and surprising — choice as the new coach in 1984. However, "Sweet Lou" turned into "Bittersweet Lou" when he bolted Minnesota for Notre Dame just one game shy of two full seasons and with a 10-12 record.

1984-1996

The Gophers won their first game under Holtz, a 31-24 decision over Rice in the Metrodome. Then the reality of the rebuilding process set in, with Minnesota losing three straight games. Two of those, however, were to top-three teams — No. 1 Nebraska and No. 3 Ohio State.

After a 33-24 win at home against Indiana, there was renewed optimism as the Gophers headed to Madison to take on the Badgers, who were 19-point favorites. Holtz and his team responded with a huge upset, knocking off Wisconsin 17-14. Foggie carried the ball 24 times for 153 yards and scored on runs of 35 and 43 yards, and Chip Lohmiller's 26-yard field goal midway through the final period was the winner. The Gopher defense shone, allowing the Badgers to cross midfield only once in the entire second half. It was Minnesota's first chance to hoist Paul Bunyan's Axe in seven years.

There would be four more losses before the next shining moment against Iowa in the season finale. Before a crowd of 63,479, the Gophers rallied for a 23-17 victory over the Hawkeyes to knock them out of Rose Bowl contention and to reclaim Floyd of Rosedale.

"It was a total team victory," Holtz said. "And it sure is good to see a hog again."

Although Holtz's first c was a tangible sense of rene

That only grew throug home victories against Wi touchdowns in each game.

Thing
when
coorc

Quarterback Rickey Foggie (14) checks out the Wisconsin defense. He stepped right in as a freshman in 1984 and paid immediate dividends with signature wins over rivals Wisconsin and Iowa. Against the Badgers, Foggie rushed for 153 yards. He still ranks among the all-time leaders in both rushing and passing yards, the only quarterback to achieve the rare double.

10 BIG GAMES REMEMBERED:
1984-1996

Oct. 13, 1984: Minnesota 17, Wisconsin 14, in Madison. It didn't take long in Lou Holtz's first season in Minnesota to have a statement game, and it came at the expense of the Badgers. Freshman quarterback Rickey Foggie scored on runs of 35 and 43 yards, and Chip Lohmiller kicked a 26-yard field goal in the fourth quarter as the Gophers shocked Wisconsin, which was favored by 19 points. It was the first win in seven years against the Badgers.

(Above) Scott Tessier (69) drags down an Iowa ball carrier as Larry Joyner (20) moves in to help. The victory over the Hawkeyes in the 1984 season finale secured another traveling trophy — Floyd of Rosedale. 'It sure is good to see a hog again," said Holtz.

Kevin Starks for a 12-yard touchdown with four minutes to go, the Gophers were in striking distance. Then they recovered a fumbled punt, but two "Hail Mary" passes fell incomplete, and Minnesota was forced to settle for a moral victory in a 13-7 defeat.

A GAIN FOR A HEADACHE

Holtz had the troops fired up for the Big Ten opener against pass-happy Purdue, and he was in rare form in a pregame pep talk. He said it was okay to give up some passing yardage as long as the defenders "put a hat" on the receivers. "We'll trade a 12-yard gain for a headache."

He even tossed in a top 10 vocabulary word: "We're gonna subjugate our [individual] welfare for the welfare of this football team."

Subjugate they did while conquering Purdue 45-15. That started a three-game Big Ten streak capped by a 22-7 win in the rain against Indiana, a game that featured some remarkable statistics. Minnesota didn't complete a single pass against the Hoosiers, but the Gophers did make three catches — interceptions by Donovan Small, Duane Dutrieuille and David Williams. Senior fullback Valdez Baylor had his best day as a Gopher, running for 141 yards and a touchdown.

1984-1996

Gophers choose

TCU's Wacker

**10 BIG GAMES REMEMBERED:
1984-1996**

Nov. 24, 1990: Minnesota 31, Iowa 24, in Minneapolis. The Gophers knocked off Rose Bowl–bound Iowa to keep Floyd of Rosedale and finish the season with a 6-5 record. Mark Smith ran 25 times for 80 yards and two touchdowns for Minnesota, while Keswic Joiner recovered a blocked punt for a touchdown and scored on a 28-yard reception to give the Gophers a 31-17 lead. Marquel Fleetwood connected on 13 of 19 passes for 159 yards and a touchdown.

At Home In Maroon And Gold

When the 1986 season arrived, there was still plenty of optimism around campus. How could there not be? The Gophers were coming off a bowl win, for starters, and they had a not only a game-breaking quarterback but a prized local running back who was about to take the football world by storm.

Darrell Thompson had been a three-sport star at John Marshall High School in Rochester, and while he could have taken his considerable talents just about anywhere in the country, he chose to stay at home.

He certainly looked at home wearing the maroon and gold. Entering the season's first game against Bowling Green, Thompson was the No. 2 tailback on the depth chart behind Ed Penn. Coming out of it, he was the talk of the town. Thompson rushed for 205 yards and four second-half touchdowns to spark a 31-7 win. The four TDs tied a team record.

Minnesota lost its next two games — 63-0 to No. 1 Oklahoma and 24-20 to Pacific — but when the Big Ten season arrived, the Gophers responded by winning three in a row against Purdue, Northwestern and Indiana. Thompson racked up 176 yards against Northwestern and another 191 against the Hoosiers.

The next two weeks were a step backward with losses at Ohio State and at home to Michigan State. But the Gophers got back on the winning track at Wisconsin, downing the Badgers 27-20. That set up a trip to Ann Arbor to face the No. 2-ranked Michigan Wolverines. Nothing would suggest Minnesota had a chance in the game, but they had a feeling.

The feeling intensified after another motivational talk the night before the game by volunteer assistant Butch Nash, whose similar speech nine years earlier had inspired the Gophers in their gigantic upset of No. 1 Michigan.

Thompson recently said the essence of Nash's message has stuck with him all these years. Nash instructed the team to "go out there and give it all you have. Leave a piece of yourself with the audience; leave it all out there on the field," Thompson said.

(Above left) The Gophers were high on the hog again in 1990 after upsetting Rose Bowl-bound Iowa. It was Minnesota's second straight win over the Hawkeyes, something the Gophers hadn't achieved in a decade. (Bottom left) Jim Wacker gives his team a pep talk at practice. When Gutekunst was let go, Minnesota lured Wacker from TCU, where he had coached for nine seasons.

Nov. 17, 1984: Minnesota 23, Iowa 17, in Minneapolis. Minnesota ended a four-game losing streak in high fashion by knocking the Hawkeyes out of Rose Bowl contention. Iowa had scored on a 95-yard punt return by Bill Happel in the third quarter, but Happel fumbled a punt late in the game that Willie Roller recovered on the Hawkeyes' 14-yard line. Gary Couch scored to give Minnesota the lead at 20-17, and Chip Lohmiller later added his third field goal of the game.

(Above) Scott Tessier (69) drags down an Iowa ball carrier as Larry Joyner (20) moves in to help. The victory over the Hawkeyes in the 1984 season finale secured another traveling trophy — Floyd of Rosedale. "It sure is good to see a hog again," said Holtz.

Kevin Starks for a 12-yard touchdown with four minutes to go, the Gophers were in striking distance. Then they recovered a fumbled punt, but two "Hail Mary" passes fell incomplete, and Minnesota was forced to settle for a moral victory in a 13-7 defeat.

A Gain For A Headache

Holtz had the troops fired up for the Big Ten opener against pass-happy Purdue, and he was in rare form in a pregame pep talk. He said it was okay to give up some passing yardage as long as the defenders "put a hat" on the receivers. "We'll trade a 12-yard gain for a headache."

He even tossed in a top 10 vocabulary word: "We're gonna subjugate our [individual] welfare for the welfare of this football team."

Subjugate they did while conquering Purdue 45-15. That started a three-game Big Ten streak capped by a 22-7 win in the rain against Indiana, a game that featured some remarkable statistics. Minnesota didn't complete a single pass against the Hoosiers, but the Gophers did make three catches — interceptions by Donovan Small, Duane Dutrieuille and David Williams. Senior fullback Valdez Baylor had his best day as a Gopher, running for 141 yards and a touchdown.

At 5-1, the Gophers jumped into the rankings at No. 20. Only problem was, they now were faced with entertaining No. 9 Ohio State.

The homecoming game against the Buckeyes was a thriller that went down to the wire. The Gophers went up 6-0 on two Lohmiller field goals, and after two touchdowns by Foggie, they were up again 19-10. But the Buckeyes came storming back to grab a 23-19 lead, and the Gophers would wind up a yard short on their comeback attempt.

The following week the Gophers fell just short against Michigan State and the nation's top rusher, Lorenzo White. Backup quarterback Alan Holt ran for two touchdowns and threw for two more, but it wasn't enough in a 31-26 loss.

Foggie was back the following week to lead the Gophers against Wisconsin in a 27-18 win in front of a Metrodome-record crowd of 64,571. For the day, he completed only three passes, but they went for 213 yards, including an 89-yarder to Mel Anderson.

Minnesota finished the season with losses to Michigan and Iowa, and a record of 6-5. But four of the five losses came against top 10 teams, and the Gophers were invited to play in the Independence Bowl on Dec. 21. It would be their first bowl appearance in eight years, which felt closer to 56 in underdog years.

BITTERSWEET LOU

More importantly, Holtz had orchestrated an amazing turnaround for a team that just two years earlier had been 1-10. Toward the end of his second season, Dome games were virtual sellouts, and the atmosphere was charged. Maybe for the first time since the Vikings arrived in 1961, University of Minnesota football was again something of a religion, and Holtz could claim many thousands of converts.

Late in November, rumors circulated that if Gerry Faust were to leave his head coaching job at Notre Dame, Holtz might be headed

(Above left) The Gophers' Mel Anderson celebrates his touchdown after a pass from Foggie in the 1985 Independence Bowl against Clemson. (Below) Players hoist the bowl trophy after the victory. The game was coach John Gutekunst's first after taking over for Holtz. He had only 16 days to prepare his charges for the contest.

10 BIG GAMES REMEMBERED: 1984-1996

Sept. 28, 1985: Oklahoma 13, Minnesota 7, in Minneapolis. Minnesota was given little chance against the No. 2 Sooners, but thanks to a stubborn bend-but-not-break defense, the Gophers had an opportunity to win in the final minutes. Rickey Foggie hit tight end Kevin Starks on a 12-yard touchdown pass with four minutes to play to get the Gophers on the board, but two last-ditch "Hail Mary" passes by Foggie failed to click on the final possession.

10 BIG GAMES REMEMBERED: 1984-1996

Dec. 21, 1985: Minnesota 20, Clemson 13, in Shreveport. John Gutekunst had only 16 days as the new head coach to prepare his team for the Independence Bowl, but the Gophers responded by notching their first bowl victory since 1962. They jumped in front 10-0 on a Chip Lohmiller field goal and a 9-yard pass from Rickey Foggie to Mel Anderson. After Clemson had taken the lead, Minnesota stormed back on another Lohmiller field goal and a 1-yard run by Valdez Baylor.

there to replace him, despite having three years left on his Minnesota contract. He did his best to try to mollify the masses without denying the possibility.

"There isn't a job in the country that I'd leave Minnesota for with the possible exception of Notre Dame," he told the *Minneapolis Star and Tribune*. "I'd be less than honest if I didn't say that I'd have to seriously consider a chance to coach at Notre Dame is it was ever offered to me."

Not only would he leave for Notre Dame, technically he could leave. There was a clause in Holtz's contract saying that if he ever was offered the Fighting Irish job, he could exit his UM contract to take it. And that's just what happened. In a span of little more than 24 hours, Faust resigned, Notre Dame offered Holtz the job and, poof, Sweet Lou was gone.

Almost overnight, Minnesotans' opinions of Holtz turned to bittersweet, if not plain bitter. His departure left many Gopher players befuddled. A number of them came out in the *Minnesota Daily* reciting a promise he made that he would stay at Minnesota until he died or got a Rose Bowl bid.

Regardless, what could have been an unsettled and uncomfortable situation was rectified quickly when Gutekunst was named the new head coach on Dec. 5. "Gutey" had the respect of players and fellow coaches alike, and many of the coaches had actively lobbied on his behalf.

But he had little time to savor his new title, because the Independence Bowl against Clemson was barely two weeks away.

No matter. The Gophers went to Shreveport and gained their first bowl victory since the 1962 Rose Bowl. They jumped ahead 10-0 on a short field goal by Lohmiller and a 9-yard Foggie-to-Anderson pass. After Clemson took the lead by scoring 13 straight points, Minnesota answered in the final period. A second field goal by Lohmiller tied it, and Baylor scored from a yard out to give Minnesota the 20-13 victory.

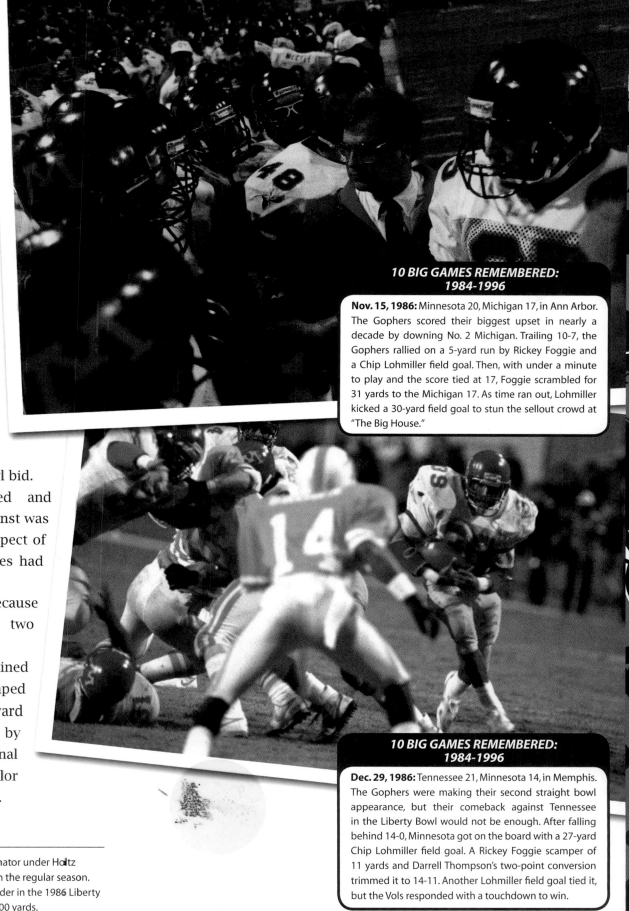

10 BIG GAMES REMEMBERED: 1984-1996

Nov. 15, 1986: Minnesota 20, Michigan 17, in Ann Arbor. The Gophers scored their biggest upset in nearly a decade by downing No. 2 Michigan. Trailing 10-7, the Gophers rallied on a 5-yard run by Rickey Foggie and a Chip Lohmiller field goal. Then, with under a minute to play and the score tied at 17, Foggie scrambled for 31 yards to the Michigan 17. As time ran out, Lohmiller kicked a 30-yard field goal to stun the sellout crowd at "The Big House."

10 BIG GAMES REMEMBERED: 1984-1996

Dec. 29, 1986: Tennessee 21, Minnesota 14, in Memphis. The Gophers were making their second straight bowl appearance, but their comeback against Tennessee in the Liberty Bowl would not be enough. After falling behind 14-0, Minnesota got on the board with a 27-yard Chip Lohmiller field goal. A Rickey Foggie scamper of 11 yards and Darrell Thompson's two-point conversion trimmed it to 14-11. Another Lohmiller field goal tied it, but the Vols responded with a touchdown to win.

(Above right) Gutekunst talks to his team on the sidelines. He was the defensive coordinator under Holtz before taking the head coaching job. He lasted six years and, in four of them, went 6-5 in the regular season. (Bottom right) Homegrown hero Darrell Thompson (39) takes aim at a Tennessee defender in the 1986 Liberty Bowl. Thompson finished his career as the school's all-time rushing leader with over 4,600 yards.

Gophers choose TCU's Wacker

10 BIG GAMES REMEMBERED: 1984-1996

Nov. 24, 1990: Minnesota 31, Iowa 24, in Minneapolis. The Gophers knocked off Rose Bowl–bound Iowa to keep Floyd of Rosedale and finish the season with a 6-5 record. Mark Smith ran 25 times for 80 yards and two touchdowns for Minnesota, while Keswic Joiner recovered a blocked punt for a touchdown and scored on a 28-yard reception to give the Gophers a 31-17 lead. Marquel Fleetwood connected on 13 of 19 passes for 159 yards and a touchdown.

AT HOME IN MAROON AND GOLD

When the 1986 season arrived, there was still plenty of optimism around campus. How could there not be? The Gophers were coming off a bowl win, for starters, and they had a not only a game-breaking quarterback but a prized local running back who was about to take the football world by storm.

Darrell Thompson had been a three-sport star at John Marshall High School in Rochester, and while he could have taken his considerable talents just about anywhere in the country, he chose to stay at home.

He certainly looked at home wearing the maroon and gold. Entering the season's first game against Bowling Green, Thompson was the No. 2 tailback on the depth chart behind Ed Penn. Coming out of it, he was the talk of the town. Thompson rushed for 205 yards and four second-half touchdowns to spark a 31-7 win. The four TDs tied a team record.

Minnesota lost its next two games — 63-0 to No. 1 Oklahoma and 24-20 to Pacific — but when the Big Ten season arrived, the Gophers responded by winning three in a row against Purdue, Northwestern and Indiana. Thompson racked up 176 yards against Northwestern and another 191 against the Hoosiers.

The next two weeks were a step backward with losses at Ohio State and at home to Michigan State. But the Gophers got back on the winning track at Wisconsin, downing the Badgers 27-20. That set up a trip to Ann Arbor to face the No. 2-ranked Michigan Wolverines. Nothing would suggest Minnesota had a chance in the game, but they had a feeling.

The feeling intensified after another motivational talk the night before the game by volunteer assistant Butch Nash, whose similar speech nine years earlier had inspired the Gophers in their gigantic upset of No. 1 Michigan.

Thompson recently said the essence of Nash's message has stuck with him all these years. Nash instructed the team to "go out there and give it all you have. Leave a piece of yourself with the audience; leave it all out there on the field," Thompson said.

(Above left) The Gophers were high on the hog again in 1990 after upsetting Rose Bowl-bound Iowa. It was Minnesota's second straight win over the Hawkeyes, something the Gophers hadn't achieved in a decade. (Bottom left) Jim Wacker gives his team a pep talk at practice. When Gutekunst was let go, Minnesota lured Wacker from TCU, where he had coached for nine seasons.

"It came to life when he started talking about the sacrifice and how one day it would be worth it."

The following day the Gophers put the lessons into play. After recovering a fumble, Minnesota scored first on a 15-yard pass from Foggie to Anderson. Michigan answered with 10 points to close the half, but the Gophers rallied with 10 of their own in the third quarter on 5-yard Foggie run and a short Lohmiller field goal after cornerback Carlos McGee had recovered another Michigan fumble.

That set the stage for the concluding drama. The Wolverines scored late in the game and elected to kick the extra point for the 17-17 tie. Then the Gophers got the ball with 2:20 remaining and mounted a drive. With 47 seconds left and the ball at the Michigan 48, Foggie dropped back to pass but couldn't find anyone open. So instead, he scrambled for 31 yards and a first down at the 17-yard line.

Thompson ran to the left for 3 yards to center the ball for Lohmiller. As time ran out, Mr. Clutch calmly drilled a 30-yard field goal to win the game 20-17. The Gophers had snapped the Wolverines' 13-game winning and 15-game unbeaten streaks, as well as their 14-game home winning streak.

THE SOUND OF SILENCE

In his *Gopher Tales* book, former announcer Ray Christensen called that game his favorite in a half century, especially the final scene in the Big House: "Over 100,000 Michigan fans sat in stunned silence, the most thrilling lack of sound I can ever remember."

The following week, Minnesota would falter 30-27 at home to Iowa, but Lohmiller again provided a highlight. His 62-yard field goal was the longest in team history. Lohmiller would go on to a great pro career with the Washington Redskins, but he would never kick a longer field goal in a game.

With a 5-3 record in the Big Ten and 6-5 overall, the Gophers finished in a tie for third place in Gutey's first season, their best finish in a decade. It was enough to earn a second straight postseason invite, this time to the Liberty Bowl.

On a cool Dec. 29 evening in Memphis, the Tennessee Volunteers showed very little southern hospitality to the northern visitors. The Vols got off to a 14-0 lead on two touchdown passes

(Above right) A demolition crew takes care to preserve some of the friezes that decorated the outer façade of Memorial Stadium. The old arena, built in 1924, stood vacant for nine years before the wrecking crew took over. (Bottom right) Wacker and four of his players grace the cover of the alumni magazine before the coach's first season in 1992. The Gophers went only 2-9 for the year.

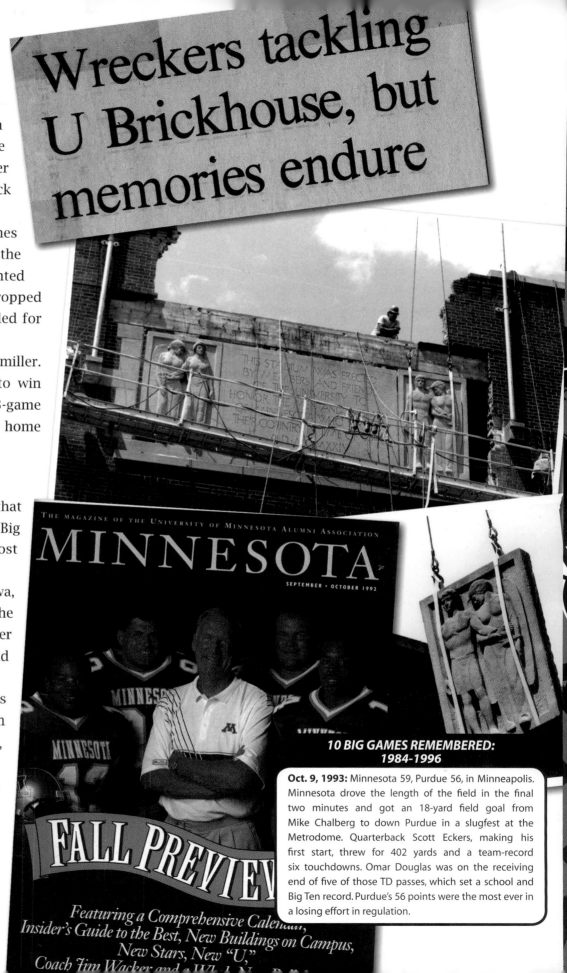

Wreckers tackling U Brickhouse, but memories endure

THE MAGAZINE OF THE UNIVERSITY OF MINNESOTA ALUMNI ASSOCIATION

MINNESOTA

SEPTEMBER · OCTOBER 1992

FALL PREVIEW

Featuring a Comprehensive Calendar, Insider's Guide to the Best, New Buildings on Campus, New Stars, New "U," Coach Jim Wacker and a Whole New...

10 BIG GAMES REMEMBERED: 1984-1996

Oct. 9, 1993: Minnesota 59, Purdue 56, in Minneapolis. Minnesota drove the length of the field in the final two minutes and got an 18-yard field goal from Mike Chalberg to down Purdue in a slugfest at the Metrodome. Quarterback Scott Eckers, making his first start, threw for 402 yards and a team-record six touchdowns. Omar Douglas was on the receiving end of five of those TD passes, which set a school and Big Ten record. Purdue's 56 points were the most ever in a losing effort in regulation.

1984-1996

by Jeff Francis before the Gophers answered with a 27-yard Lohmiller field goal right before half.

In the second half, Minnesota continued its momentum, climbing to within 14-11 on an 11-yard Foggie run and two-point conversion by Thompson. When Lohmiller kicked a 25-yard chip shot early in the fourth quarter, the Gophers had knotted the game at 14. But Tennessee answered on its next drive with another Francis touchdown pass to Joey Clinkscales, and the Vols held on for the 21-14 victory in front of 51,327.

Gutey's Gophers came out like gangbusters in 1987, rolling up five straight victories over Northern Iowa, California, Central Michigan, Purdue and Northwestern. But just when hopes were soaring, the five-game streak was negated by a four-game skid.

The last of those losses came in another memorable game with Michigan. In the second quarter, Thompson took a handoff in his own end zone on a draw, picked up a block from Marcus Evans on about the 5-yard line and took off down the right sideline. Ninety-eight yards later, he had the longest run in Big Ten history.

The Gophers grabbed a 17-7 lead and were thinking of their second straight Little Brown Jug victory, but the Wolverines stormed back to win 30-20. Thompson wound up with two touchdowns and 201 yards, the most ever allowed by a Michigan team.

That '87 season would end with another 6-5 record but only 3-5 in the Big Ten. Foggie finished his career with 5,162 passing yards and 7,312 yards of total offense, both Minnesota records. And after just two seasons, Thompson's numbers were sterling: 2,649 yards and 21 touchdowns. He became the first back in Big Ten history to run for more than 1,000 yards in his freshman and sophomore years, and his name was being pitched as a Heisman Trophy candidate.

Although Thompson's career continued to flourish, a Heisman never materialized. Meanwhile, the Gophers' fortunes took a turn for the

---

**10 BIG GAMES REMEMBERED:
1984-1996**

Oct. 7, 1995: Minnesota 39, Purdue 38, in Minneapolis. Senior Chris Darkins rushed for a school-record 294 yards and three touchdowns as the Gophers beat the Boilermakers in the third straight shootout between the two teams. Darkins gained 232 yards on 23 carries in the second half alone. Cory Sauter's pass to Ryan Thelwell on a two-point conversion provided the final margin. In three games, the teams combined for 278 points and 3,356 yards.

(Left) Chris Darkins dashes for some of his school-record 294 yards against Purdue in 1995. Darkins was one of a long line of standout running backs for the Gophers in the 1990s and 2000s. Of the top 10 all-time rushers, eight came from that time period. (Opposite page) Tyrone Carter scoops up one of the two fumbles he returned for scores against Syracuse, setting an NCAA record in 1996. Carter is one of the most honored Gopher defenders ever — twice an All-American and the 1999 Jim Thorpe Award winner as the nation's top defensive back.

worse. The 1988 campaign produced only two ties in Big Ten play, versus Northwestern and Illinois, and an overall mark of 2-7-2.

The following two seasons brought records of 6-5, with the Gophers unable to get over the hump to another bowl invitation. Thompson's illustrious career would come to an end in 1989. He would go into Minnesota's record books with 936 carries, 4,654 yards and 40 touchdowns — marks that have stood the test of time.

In 1990, Minnesota won its sixth game in the last seven tries against Wisconsin and finished the season with a rousing 31-24 home win over Rose Bowl-bound Iowa in front of 64,694 fans. It would be the last big win for Gutekunst.

The following season, after a 2-9 mark and last-place Big Ten finish, he was let go. Despite an overall record of 29-37-2, Gutey had left a positive mark. In six seasons, he had finished .500 or better four times, led his team to a second consecutive bowl bid and finished the 1986 season tied for third in the Big Ten — a standing Minnesota has yet to match.

STRUGGLING TO FIND SUCCESS

Gutekunst was replaced by Jim Wacker. The 57-year-old Wacker had been a head coach for 21 years — the last nine at Texas Christian University — and his overall record was 144-91-3. Outgoing and enthusiastic like Holtz, he was known as being a good recruiter.

Wacker would indeed bring a number of talented players to Minnesota, but his teams struggled to find success on the field, finishing no higher than eighth in the Big Ten.

The best season was 1993 when the 4-7 Gophers were led by sophomore running back Chris Darkins and quarterbacks Tim Schade and Scott Eckers.

In the first two games of the season — a 38-20 loss at No. 17 Penn State and a 27-10 win at home against Indiana State — Schade threw for a combined 823 yards, a team record for a two-game stretch. His 478 yards against Penn State is also a record.

Minnesota then lost three games in a row before a midseason matchup with Purdue at the Metrodome — a game that could only be described as flat-out crazy. The Golden Gophers, on the strength of a last-second 18-yard field goal by Mike Chalberg, beat the Boilermakers 59-56. Needless to say, a number of records were set.

Eckers, a junior from St. Louis Park who was making his first start, threw for 402 yards and a school-record six touchdown passes. Senior receiver Omar Douglas had eight catches for 149 yards and five touchdowns, the latter a Minnesota and Big Ten record. And Purdue's 56 points were the most ever by a losing team in Division I-A history.

"It was the wildest and hairiest game I've ever been in," said Wacker after the game. "It was agony, and then ecstasy. It was just crazy."

10 BIG GAMES REMEMBERED: 1984-1996

Sept. 21, 1996: Minnesota 35, Syracuse 33, in Minneapolis. A 26-yard field goal by Adam Bailey with 42 seconds remaining lifted Minnesota over Donovan McNabb and Syracuse. The teams combined for 11 turnovers. Minnesota trailed 12-7 when freshman safety Tyrone Carter picked up a fumble and raced 63 yards for a touchdown. Less than a minute later, Carter set an NCAA record by returning a second fumble for a touchdown.

The two teams had so much fun running up and down the field that they decided to do it again the next two years. In 1994, Purdue prevailed 49-37 in a slugfest in West Lafayette, and back in Minnesota the next year the Gophers won another squeaker 39-38. It took a two-point conversion from quarterback Cory Sauter to Ryan Thelwell with 1:38 remaining to seal the deal in that one.

Darkins ran wild in that 1995 game with 34 carries for a Minnesota-record 294 yards and three touchdowns. In the second half alone he gained 232 yards on 23 carries.

The totals for the three games put together are even crazier. The two teams combined for 278 points and 3,356 yards. Purdue running back Mike Alstott, who scored three touchdowns against the Gophers in 1995, finished his career with 13 touchdowns against Minnesota.

SHORT ONE COMMODITY

Wacker's teams had two big upsets of ranked opponents. In '93, the Gophers beat No. 15 and Rose Bowl-bound Wisconsin 28-21 in front of a packed house at the Metrodome. In 1996, Wacker's final season, Minnesota downed quarterback Donovan McNabb and No. 23 Syracuse 35-33 on Adam Bailey's 26-yard field goal with 42 seconds left.

Against the Orange, Sauter's touchdown pass to Tutu Atwell got the Gophers on the board first, and then after falling behind 12-7, they surged ahead again on the strength of two fumble returns for touchdowns by freshman safety Tyrone Carter in a span of 56 seconds in the third quarter. The big plays served as a coming-out party for Carter, who would go on to become a two-time All-American.

The win against Syracuse gave Wacker his best start at 3-0, but it was all downhill from there, and when the season ended with a ninth-place Big Ten finish, Wacker was finished.

His five-season record was only 16-39, but he did produce the most Academic All-Big Ten players over a three-year span and managed to raise attendance figures at the Metrodome considerably.

With Holtz, Gutey and Wacker, the Gophers had employed three coaches with divergent personalities who gave equal parts heart, soul and energy. Unfortunately, the Gophers were shy on the most precious commodity — game-breaking, season-making talent — with not a single first-team All-American. And that was reflected in the collective record of 55-87-2 from 1984 to 1996.

It was time to turn things around once again.

(Above) Paul Bunyan's Axe stands above the crowd after the Gophers beat Wisconsin in 1994. The axe goes to the winner of major college football's longest-standing rivalry — 117 years and counting. (Opposite page) Wacker leads his team off the Metrodome field after a Minnesota win. In his five years as head coach, Wacker managed only a 16-39 record.

NEXT: Ups, downs and magical moments. The rebuilder. A rare win in Columbus. The posse catches up. New hope, new home.

Ups, Downs And Magic Moments

1997-2007
Record: 65 wins, 68 losses

"In college football today, the difference between finishing 8-3 and 3-8 is so small that if you blink your eye, you might miss it."

— Coach Glen Mason in 1999

Glen Mason was named the 25th head coach of the Golden Gophers on Dec. 14, 1996. He came to Minnesota with a reputation of being able to turn programs around, a feat he accomplished both at Kent State and at Kansas.

The former player and assistant coach at Ohio State had a record of 12-10 in two years at Kent State, helping it to its first winning season in a decade. At Kansas, he lifted the Jayhawks out of disarray and to two Aloha Bowls.

He would be a perfect fit, since Minnesota's football program was in need of a Mason with good rebuilding skills.

His first season in 1997 was the classic transition year, long on positive signs but short on results. After an opening loss at Hawaii, Mason notched his first victory in Week 2 with a 53-29 romp over Iowa State. Another win followed at Memphis before times turned lean.

The Gophers lost eight of their final nine to finish 3-9, but to some extent the losses were deceiving. There were two near misses in back-to-back games — a 16-15 loss at No. 1 Penn State and a 22-21 loss at home to Wisconsin.

Lamanzer Williams led the nation in sacks with 18.5 and was named to the All-America team. He became the first Gopher to win that honor since Doug Kingsriter in 1971 — a span of 26 years.

The following season brought Big Ten victories against Michigan State and Iowa, and an overall record of 5-6.

This time it was junior safety Tyrone Carter's turn to be named an All-American after collecting 158 tackles for the season. Carter, from Pompano Beach, Florida, was only 5-foot-9 and 184 pounds but played much bigger. He was a fierce, old-fashioned tackler, hitting low and often finishing by lifting up the ball carrier and depositing him on his backside. He also returned punts and kickoffs.

GETTING DEFENSIVE

Although Mason's teams would become known for their prolific offense, it was the defense that initially keyed the team's move up the standings.

The Gophers ranked 11th in the Big Ten and 104th in the nation in rushing defense the year before Mason arrived, allowing a whopping 246.5 yards per game. But in '98, they ranked fourth in the Big Ten and

---

(Preceding page) Glen Mason and his team celebrate a tight 1998 victory over Michigan State in the Metrodome. It had been a long dry spell against the Spartans, as the Gophers had not defeated MSU since 1976. (Right) Mason came to Minnesota with a reputation of rebuilding downtrodden programs. He pretty much stayed true to form, taking the Gophers to bowl games in seven of his 10 years and posting the first career winning record by a Minnesota coach since Murray Warmath retired in 1971.

1997-2007

13th in nation while allowing just 103.7 yards per game on the ground.

The Gophers were poised to make a move in 1999 if they could catch some breaks, and Mason was eerily prescient before the season.

"In college football today, the difference between finishing 8-3 and 3-8 is so small that if you blink your eye, you might miss it. The key for us this season is not to blink."

Apparently, they didn't blink. For the second straight year the Gophers swept their non-conferences games, then started the Big Ten season with a 33-14 win at Northwestern. The start turned some heads, and Minnesota made its first appearance in the national ratings since 1985 at No. 25 in the AP poll.

Then came a 20-17 overtime loss to No. 20 Wisconsin, and after a 37-7 win at Illinois, two more close losses to No. 22 Ohio State 20-17 and No. 18 Purdue 33-28. The Gophers were on the brink of excellence; they just needed a signature win to catapult them to new heights.

That came the following week against Penn State in Happy Valley, the site of despair two years earlier when Minnesota lost the 16-15 squeaker. This time around, Joe Paterno's Nittany Lions were ranked No. 2, dreaming of a national title and favored by two touchdowns.

Minnesota's Thomas Hamner was the workhorse, gaining 96 yards in 38 carries and adding three catches for 58 yards. His 49-yard touchdown gave the Gophers a 21-20 lead in the fourth quarter, but Penn State answered with a field goal.

The Gophers would have one more chance with 1:50 remaining and the ball on their 20-yard line. Mason went for broke right away, as Billy Cockerham threw a bomb down the right sideline that Ron Johnson hauled in for a 46-yard gain. Three plays later, Minnesota had fourth-and-10 at the PSU 40. Up flew a "Hail Mary" pass, and the prayer was answered. The ball bounced off Johnson's chest, and as gravity was about to complete its task, Arland Bruce swept in to catch the ball deep in Penn State territory.

"After Ron tipped it, I just saw the ball hanging in the air saying, like, 'Come get me! Come get me!'" Bruce said.

That gave freshman kicker Dan Nystrom a chance to be the hero, and he seized upon it. His 32-yard field goal as time expired gave the Gophers their first huge win in more than a decade.

ENDING A 32-YEAR DROUGHT

The momentum carried over to the final two games — victories over Indiana and Iowa — and at season's end the Gophers stood at 8-3 with their first bowl game since 1986 on the horizon. And

Nov. 6 1999: Minnesota 24, Penn State 23, in State College. Two years earlier, the Gophers almost knocked off No. 1 Penn State, and this time around they didn't miss the opportunity. The No. 2 Nittany Lions took a 23-21 lead with 1:50 to play. Minnesota's improbable drive included a 46-yard bomb from Billy Cockerham to Ron Johnson and a "Hail Mary" pass that Johnson deflected to Arland Bruce. Dan Nystrom then kicked the game-winning 32-yard field goal.

(Preceding page) Dan Nystrom (28) reacts to his game-winning field goal against Penn State in 1999. Nystrom, the Gophers' all-time leading scorer, kicked a Big Ten-record 71 field goals in his career. (Below) Minnesota players swarm the field after the upset of the Nittany Lions in their own den in '99. Alex Hass (84) gives Mason a boost during the celebration.

1997-2007

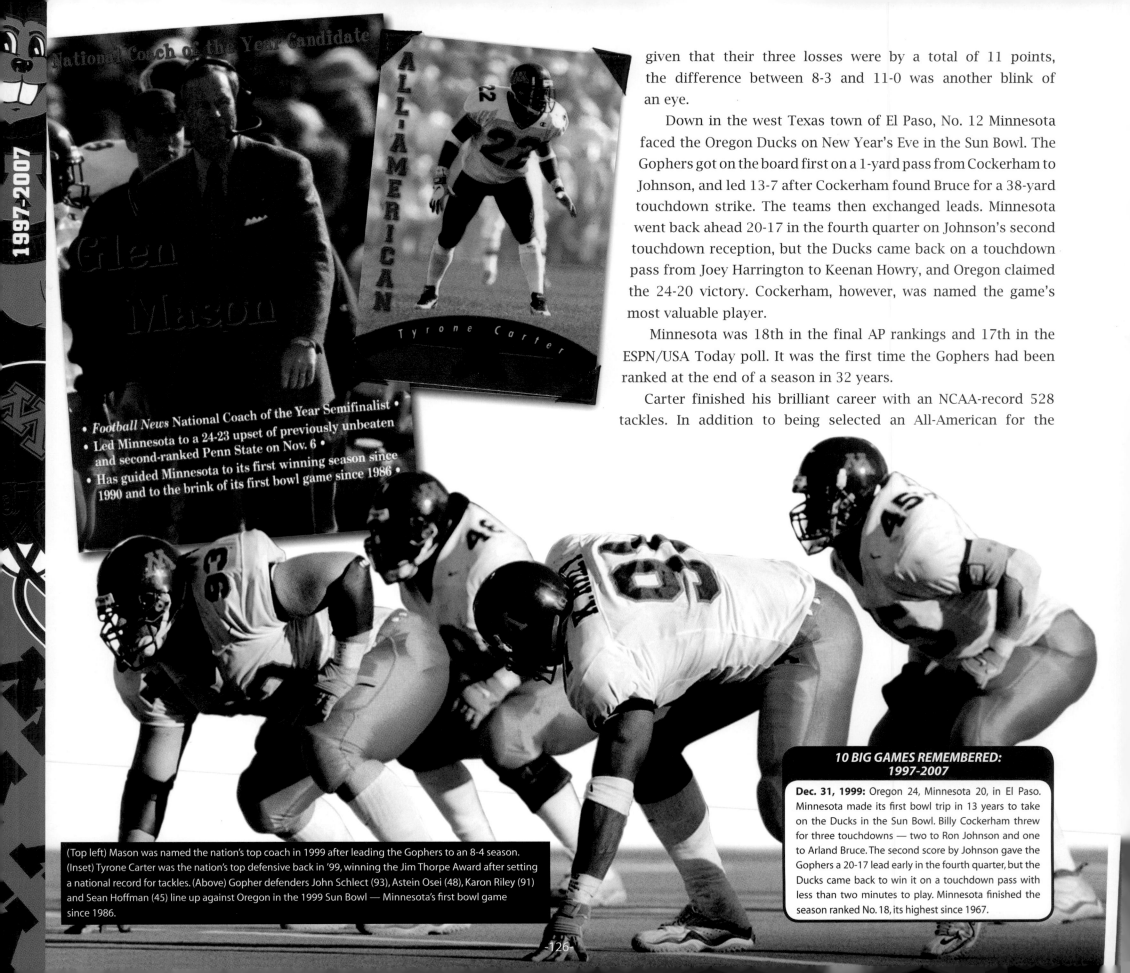

National Coach of the Year Candidate

Glen Mason

ALL-AMERICAN

Tyrone Carter

- *Football News* National Coach of the Year Semifinalist •
- Led Minnesota to a 24-23 upset of previously unbeaten and second-ranked Penn State on Nov. 6 •
- Has guided Minnesota to its first winning season since 1990 and to the brink of its first bowl game since 1986 •

given that their three losses were by a total of 11 points, the difference between 8-3 and 11-0 was another blink of an eye.

Down in the west Texas town of El Paso, No. 12 Minnesota faced the Oregon Ducks on New Year's Eve in the Sun Bowl. The Gophers got on the board first on a 1-yard pass from Cockerham to Johnson, and led 13-7 after Cockerham found Bruce for a 38-yard touchdown strike. The teams then exchanged leads. Minnesota went back ahead 20-17 in the fourth quarter on Johnson's second touchdown reception, but the Ducks came back on a touchdown pass from Joey Harrington to Keenan Howry, and Oregon claimed the 24-20 victory. Cockerham, however, was named the game's most valuable player.

Minnesota was 18th in the final AP rankings and 17th in the ESPN/USA Today poll. It was the first time the Gophers had been ranked at the end of a season in 32 years.

Carter finished his brilliant career with an NCAA-record 528 tackles. In addition to being selected an All-American for the

10 BIG GAMES REMEMBERED: 1997-2007

Dec. 31, 1999: Oregon 24, Minnesota 20, in El Paso. Minnesota made its first bowl trip in 13 years to take on the Ducks in the Sun Bowl. Billy Cockerham threw for three touchdowns — two to Ron Johnson and one to Arland Bruce. The second score by Johnson gave the Gophers a 20-17 lead early in the fourth quarter, but the Ducks came back to win it on a touchdown pass with less than two minutes to play. Minnesota finished the season ranked No. 18, its highest since 1967.

(Top left) Mason was named the nation's top coach in 1999 after leading the Gophers to an 8-4 season. (Inset) Tyrone Carter was the nation's top defensive back in '99, winning the Jim Thorpe Award after setting a national record for tackles. (Above) Gopher defenders John Schlect (93), Astein Osei (48), Karon Riley (91) and Sean Hoffman (45) line up against Oregon in the 1999 Sun Bowl — Minnesota's first bowl game since 1986.

second straight year, Carter received the Jim Thorpe Award as the nation's top defensive back.

He was joined on the All-America team by center Ben Hamilton. And Mason? In just his third year, he was selected by the *Football News* as the Coach of the Year.

Hamner finished his career with 3,810 yards. He would give way to a seemingly endless parade of superb backs in the first decade of the new century: Tellis Redmon, Thomas Tapeh, Marion Barber III, Terry Jackson Jr., Laurence Maroney, Gary Russell and Amir Pinnix.

10 BIG GAMES REMEMBERED: 1997-2007

Oct. 14, 2000: Minnesota 29, Ohio State 17, in Columbus. The Gophers took down No. 6 Ohio State to move into a four-way tie for first place in the Big Ten. It was the first time Minnesota had won in Columbus since 1949 — a span of 51 years and 10 presidents. The Gophers racked up 381 yards against the league's top defense. Tellis Redmon ran for 118 yards and a score, and Ron Johnson caught eight balls for 163 yards and his 18th career touchdown, a team record.

A Rare Win In Columbus

The Gophers followed their remarkable 1999 season with another good year by finishing 6-6 in 2000, and for the second straight year they had a huge win on the road, this time against No. 6 Ohio State.

Coming into the OSU game as an 11-point underdog, Minnesota had a field day against the Big Ten's top defense, gaining 381 yards. Travis Cole had a strong game at quarterback, Redmon ran for 118 yards and a touchdown, and Johnson grabbed eight balls for 163 yards and his 18th career receiving touchdown, a school record.

The Gophers whipped the Buckeyes 29-17 for their first victory in Columbus since 1949 — a span of 51 years. The win put Minnesota at 3-1 and in a three-way tie for first in the Big Ten.

Dreams of a trip to Pasadena were short-lived, however, as the Gophers dropped their next three games to Indiana, Northwestern and Wisconsin. But a 27-24 victory in the final game against Iowa qualified them for a second straight postseason game — the Micronpc.com Bowl against North Carolina State.

The Golden Gophers came out smoking in Fort Lauderdale against the Wolfpack. They turned an early interception by Justin Hall into six points and added two more touchdowns in the first quarter. But by the time the lead reached 24-0, North Carolina State awoke and came storming back, outscoring Minnesota 30-6 in the second half for a 38-30 win. Redmon was the offensive star, carrying the ball 42 times for a Micronpc.com Bowl-record 246 yards.

At the season's end, Hamilton was again selected as an All-American, and he was joined by punter Preston Gruening, who averaged 44.5 yards per boot.

With nine new defensive starters and a rebuilt offensive line, Minnesota slipped to 4-7 overall in 2001 but salvaged Paul Bunyan's Axe in the season finale against Wisconsin. Marion

(Above right) The scoreboard tells the tale in 2000 in Columbus. The last time Minnesota won there was in 1949, when the leading rusher was Billy Bye and the team MVP was Bud Grant. (Right) The Gophers went to Miami in 2000 for their second straight bowl trip, this time the Micronpc.com Bowl. It was the first time the team had been to back-to-back bowl games since 1961-62.

10 BIG GAMES REMEMBERED:
1997-2007

Dec. 30, 2002: Minnesota 29, Arkansas 14, in Nashville. Minnesota made its first of three appearances in the Music City Bowl and whipped No. 25 Arkansas. The Gophers spotted the Razorbacks an early touchdown, but then stormed back to score 29 straight points. Dan Nystrom had five field goals, Ben Utecht scored on a 19-yard pass from Asad Abdul-Khaliq and Thomas Tapeh added a 33-yard touchdown run. Nystrom finished his career with 71 field goals, a Big Ten record.

Barber III — son of former Gophers star Marion Barber Jr. — showed flashes of his later brilliance in the second game against Louisiana-Lafayette by rushing for 173 yards in a 44-14 win.

ON THE REBOUND

The Gophers were on the rebound in 2002, winning all five non-conference games en route to an 8-5 record. After a midseason three-game winning streak, the 23rd-ranked Gophers fell 34-3 to No. 6 Ohio State, which started a four-game slide to end the season.

But they were back in a bowl again, this time for the first of the team's three trips to Nashville for the Music City Bowl. The Gophers were finely tuned and outplayed No. 25 Arkansas 29-14.

(Left) Quarterback Asad Abdul-Khaliq finished his career in 2002 as the leading passer in school history and still ranks third. (Above) Michael Lehan, Nystrom and Abdul-Khaliq after the 2002 Music City Bowl victory over Arkansas. Nystrom booted five field goals and was named the game's MVP.

The 2003 season had more than its share of ups, downs and milestones. The Gophers stormed to six straight victories while outscoring opponents 249-82. Coupled with the bowl victory against Arkansas, that made for a seven-game winning streak, the longest since 1961.

Barber and Maroney were a dynamic duo, and by season's end they would combine for a dozen 100-yard rushing games. Meanwhile, Asad Abdul-Khaliq was having a banner year at quarterback, with Jared Ellerson and Aaron Hosack being his favorite targets.

By the time Michigan came to town in mid-October, the Gophers were ranked No. 17 and the Wolverines No. 20. Some 62,000 fans packed the Metrodome on a Friday evening for the nationally televised contest, and for a majority of the game, the Gophers put on one of their best shows. After three quarters, the score stood Minnesota 28, Michigan 7. That's when the bottom fell out. The Wolverines somehow managed to outscore the Gophers 31-7 in the fourth quarter to come back for a remarkable but gut-wrenching 38-35 victory.

Another heartbreaker followed the next week — a 44-38 home loss to No. 15 Michigan State — and what seemed to be an inevitable march to a high-tier bowl had suddenly taken a detour. But the team did get back on track, beating Illinois, Indiana and Wisconsin, the latter on a last-second field goal by Rhys Lloyd.

BACK TO EL PASO

A loss to Iowa in the season's last week sealed the Gophers' destiny: a return trip to the Sun Bowl in El Paso and a repeat matchup with Oregon, their 1999 opponent.

Center Greg Eslinger (61) was the anchor of the Gophers' offensive line that also included Mark Setterstrom (68) and Jeremiah Carter (69). Eslinger and Setterstrom were freshmen in 2002, but both went on to be named All-Americans. Eslinger was selected All-America twice, and won the Rimington Trophy as the nation's top center and the Outland Trophy as the top lineman when he was a senior.

10 BIG GAMES REMEMBERED:
1997-2007

Oct. 10, 2003: Michigan 38, Minnesota 35, in Minneapolis. The Gophers came into the contest ranked No. 17 and with a seven-game winning streak — their longest since 1961. More than 62,000 fans packed the Metrodome to watch them dominate No. 20 Michigan through three quarters. But the 28-7 lead disintegrated in a remarkable fourth quarter in which the Wolverines outscored Minnesota 31-7 on the 100th anniversary of the Little Brown Jug.

(Above) Laurence Maroney (22) teamed up with Marion Barber III to form the most productive running back tandem in Gopher history. Maroney is second on Minnesota's all-time rushing list, while Barber is fourth. Both have since gone on to productive pro careers — Maroney with the New England Patriots and Barber with the Dallas Cowboys.

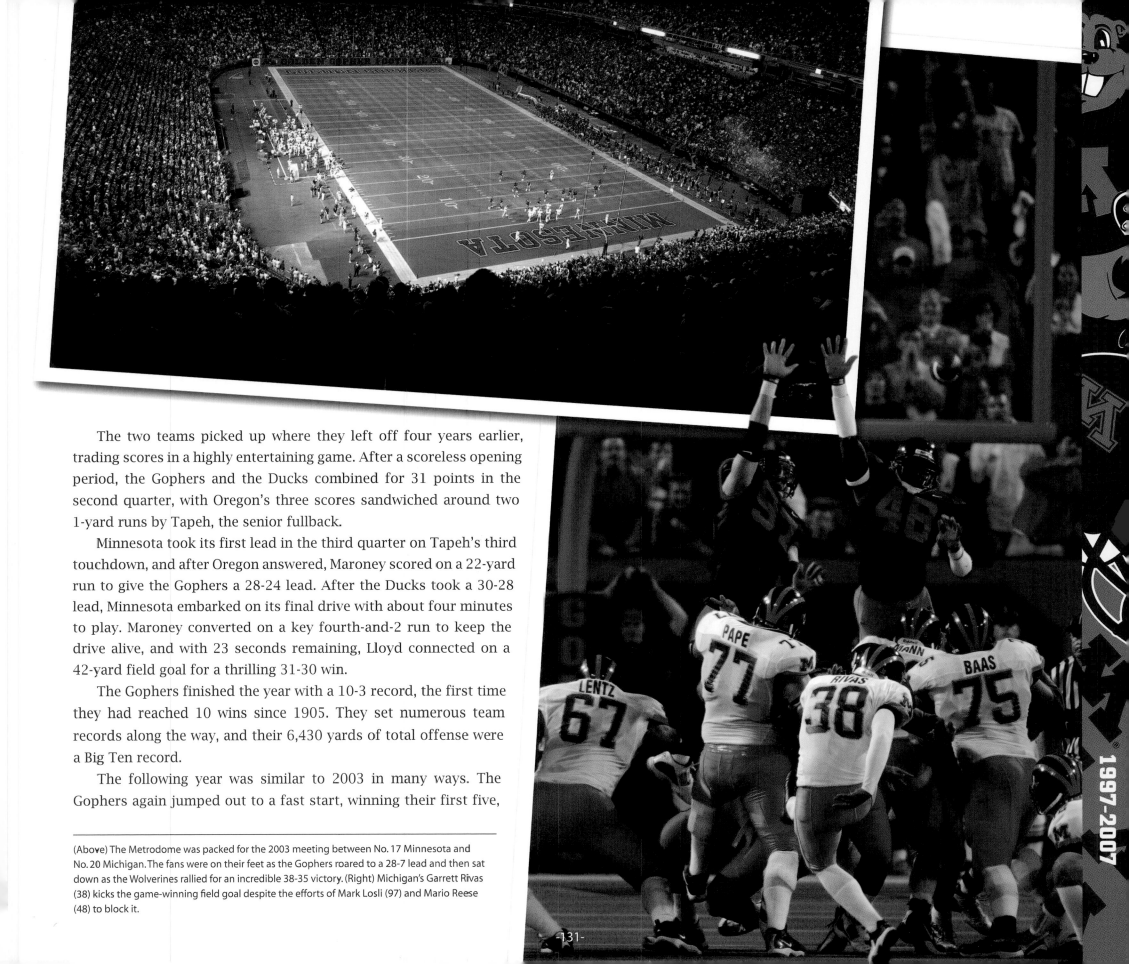

The two teams picked up where they left off four years earlier, trading scores in a highly entertaining game. After a scoreless opening period, the Gophers and the Ducks combined for 31 points in the second quarter, with Oregon's three scores sandwiched around two 1-yard runs by Tapeh, the senior fullback.

Minnesota took its first lead in the third quarter on Tapeh's third touchdown, and after Oregon answered, Maroney scored on a 22-yard run to give the Gophers a 28-24 lead. After the Ducks took a 30-28 lead, Minnesota embarked on its final drive with about four minutes to play. Maroney converted on a key fourth-and-2 run to keep the drive alive, and with 23 seconds remaining, Lloyd connected on a 42-yard field goal for a thrilling 31-30 win.

The Gophers finished the year with a 10-3 record, the first time they had reached 10 wins since 1905. They set numerous team records along the way, and their 6,430 yards of total offense were a Big Ten record.

The following year was similar to 2003 in many ways. The Gophers again jumped out to a fast start, winning their first five,

(Above) The Metrodome was packed for the 2003 meeting between No. 17 Minnesota and No. 20 Michigan. The fans were on their feet as the Gophers roared to a 28-7 lead and then sat down as the Wolverines rallied for an incredible 38-35 victory. (Right) Michigan's Garrett Rivas (38) kicks the game-winning field goal despite the efforts of Mark Losli (97) and Mario Reese (48) to block it.

1997-2007

and headed into a game at Michigan ranked No. 13 while the Wolverines were No. 14. And again, Minnesota came tantalizingly close to winning the Little Brown Jug, but Michigan rallied late to win 27-24.

For the second consecutive season, Maroney and Barber had defenses seeing stars. Literally. The stellar tandem combined for 2,617 yards, 23 rushing touchdowns and 13 100-yard games. It was the first time in NCAA history that two backs from the same team had each run for 1,000 yards in consecutive seasons. With the holes provided by the offensive line — led by

All-Americans Greg Eslinger and Mark Setterstrom — and their breakaway speed, any off-tackle run could go the distance, and many did.

The Gophers finished 6-5 and, for the second time in three years, received an invitation to play in the Music City Bowl. This time the opponent was Alabama, and the Gophers again found Nashville to their liking.

The Crimson Tide hadn't allowed a single back to rush for 100 yards during the season, but they hadn't yet played Minnesota. Barber rambled

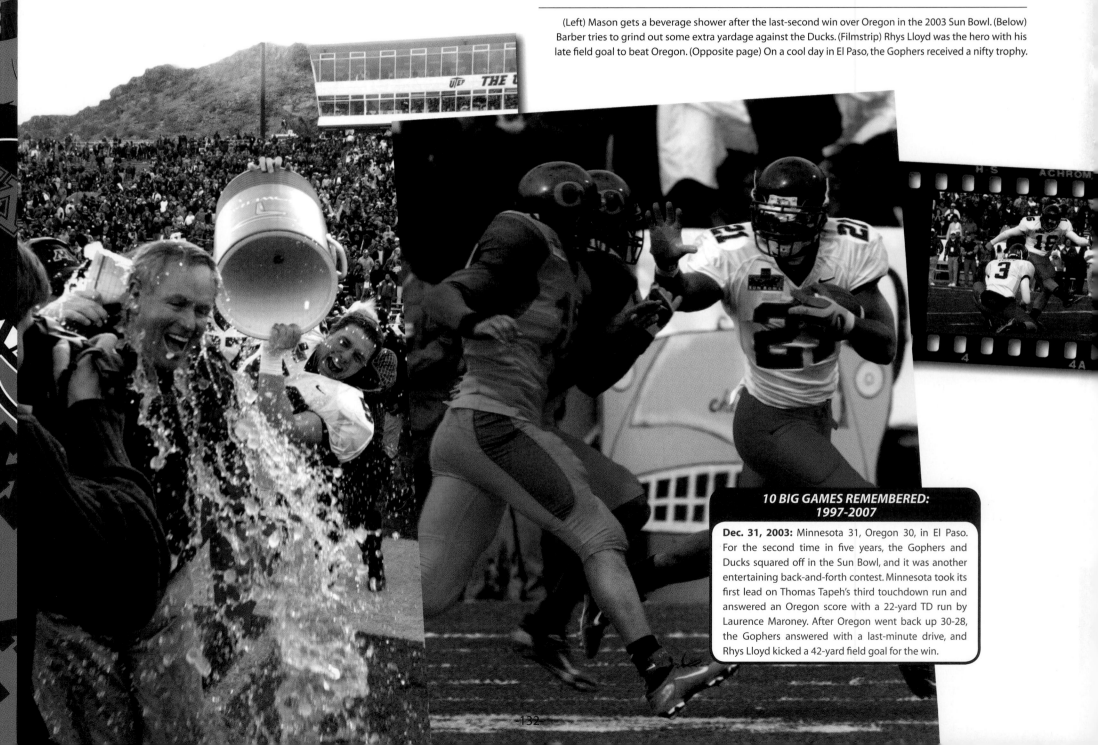

(Left) Mason gets a beverage shower after the last-second win over Oregon in the 2003 Sun Bowl. (Below) Barber tries to grind out some extra yardage against the Ducks. (Filmstrip) Rhys Lloyd was the hero with his late field goal to beat Oregon. (Opposite page) On a cool day in El Paso, the Gophers received a nifty trophy.

10 BIG GAMES REMEMBERED: 1997-2007

Dec. 31, 2003: Minnesota 31, Oregon 30, in El Paso. For the second time in five years, the Gophers and Ducks squared off in the Sun Bowl, and it was another entertaining back-and-forth contest. Minnesota took its first lead on Thomas Tapeh's third touchdown run and answered an Oregon score with a 22-yard TD run by Laurence Maroney. After Oregon went back up 30-28, the Gophers answered with a last-minute drive, and Rhys Lloyd kicked a 42-yard field goal for the win.

SUN BOWL CHAMPIONS

MINNESOTA

1997-2007

for 187 yards and a touchdown in his final game as a Gopher, while Maroney added 105 yards as the Gophers downed Alabama 20-16 in front of 66,089 fans.

UNEXPECTED MAGIC

With Barber gone in 2005, Maroney needed a new running mate, and Gary Russell stepped up in style, setting the team record with 19 rushing touchdowns.

The conference season opened with a thrilling 42-35 double-overtime win against No. 11 Purdue at the Metrodome. The following week, the

No. 18 Gophers traveled to Penn State in the hopes of continuing their streak of four straight Governor's Victory Bell wins. The Nittany Lions had other thoughts, and pounced on Minnesota 44-14.

Fans had little reason to expect any magic seven days later in Ann Arbor. So, of course, the Golden Gophers responded by pulling a gigantic rabbit out of a hat in front of 111,117 fans at "The Big House."

The Gophers were tied with Michigan at 20-20 with under three minutes remaining and the ball on their own 12. But starting quarterback Bryan Cupito was on the bench with ice bags on both shoulders and his eyes glazed from a mild concussion. So the game plan was simple: Hand the ball off and roll the dice in overtime. But then on third-and-10 from the 26, Russell found a seam down the right sideline, picked up blocks by Ellerson

(Below) Marion Barber III (21) followed in his father's footsteps as a star at Minnesota. Barber, the son, is fourth on the Gophers' all-time yardage list, while his father ranks sixth.

and tight end Matt Spaeth and rambled 61 yards to the Michigan 13. Three plays later, with one second remaining, Jason Giannini split the uprights on a 30-yard field goal.

A moment later, the players raced across the field in search of the Little Brown Jug, a trophy the Gophers last hoisted in 1986, which was before some players on the team were even born.

That emotional high lasted seven days and three-plus quarters, through the process

10 BIG GAMES REMEMBERED: 1997-2007

Dec. 31, 2004: Minnesota 20, Alabama 16, in Nashville. The tandem of Marion Barber III and Laurence Maroney combined for nearly 300 yards rushing as Minnesota beat Alabama to win the Music City Bowl before a record crowd of 66,089. The Crimson Tide had not allowed a single back to rush for 100 yards, a stat the Gophers used for motivation. Barber wound up with 37 carries for 187 yards and a touchdown, and Maroney tacked on 105 yards in 29 carries.

GAYLORD HOTELS

MUSIC CITY BOWL

PRESENTED BY

BRIDGESTONE

UNIVERSITY OF MINNESOTA
GOLDEN GOPHERS
2004 CHAMPIONS

(Above) Mason leads the cheers after Minnesota beat Alabama in 2004. The game was the second of three trips to Nashville for the Music City Bowl. The Gophers won two of the three.

**10 BIG GAMES REMEMBERED:
1997-2007**

Sept. 24, 2005: Minnesota 42, Purdue 35, in Minneapolis. The Gophers' season got a big boost with a thrilling double-overtime victory over No. 11 Purdue. Minnesota trailed 28-20 late in the game when Bryan Cupito connected with tight end Matt Spaeth for an 8-yard touchdown. On the two-point conversion, Cupito kept the ball himself and edged into the end zone. The teams traded touchdowns in the first overtime, and Gary Russell's 3-yard scoring run won it.

Bryan Cupito (3) slices into the end zone for a two-point conversion to tie Purdue in a wild overtime shootout in 2005. Cupito was actually much better known for his throwing ability, as he is the Gophers' career leader in passing yardage and touchdown passes. However, Cupito will soon be feeling the heat from Adam Weber, who as a freshman in 2007 set single-season records for yards, completions and touchdown passes.

of building a seemingly secure 34-24 lead against Wisconsin in a showdown at the Metrodome. But then came another bitter fourth-quarter pill. First, the Badgers scored to pull within three points, and as time was winding down, they blocked a punt after a fumbled snap. When the Badgers pounced on the ball in the end zone to secure a 38-34 win, Minnesota's fortunes had taken another dramatic turn, despite 258 yards from Maroney.

The team finished 7-5 after a 34-31 loss to Virginia in another Music City Bowl, but the sting of a few defeats couldn't overshadow what had become a truly remarkable run in the Mason era: the Gophers averaged 498 yards per game on offense, the third-highest total of all time in the Big Ten; they became the only team in the nation to both run and pass for at least 2,000 yards in each of seven seasons; and they became the first team in NCAA history to have two players each run for 1,000-plus yards in three consecutive seasons.

Maroney was an All-America pick and Eslinger raked in the hardware. In addition to All-America honors for the second straight year, Eslinger won the Rimington Trophy as the nation's outstanding center and the Outland Trophy as the best interior lineman.

THE POSSE CATCHES UP

I sat down with Mason before the start of the 2006 season and asked him to reflect on his tenure. At that point, his record was 58-50 at Minnesota, his contract had been extended and athletic director Joel Maturi had recently suggested that the football team was not far away from a Big Ten title — the grail that had been elusive for nearly four decades.

"We've made a lot of progress," Mason said. "We've been a blink of an eye away from really being a serious contender on a number of occasions. But until you do it, you haven't done it.

"All you have to do is look at the money that people are investing in their programs in the way of football-related facilities and it's almost mind-boggling. And that's because there's an *intense* race to be in position to win Big Ten championships."

The intense race in 2006 did not involve the Gophers. When a 44-0 loss to No. 1 Ohio State dropped them to 3-6, it looked as if the string of bowl appearances was coming to a close. But instead, the Gophers rallied to beat Indiana, Michigan State and Iowa to finish at 6-6 and earn an invitation to the Insight Bowl in Tempe, Arizona.

HOMECOMING: CENTER STAGE
September 17-24, 2005

UNIVERSITY OF MINNESOTA
GOPHER FOOTBALL
2006 INSIGHT BOWL

Insight BOWL
TEMPE ▾ ARIZONA

1997-2007

The Insight Bowl was Mason's last game as the head coach at Minnesota. He finished with a 64-57 record over 10 seasons.

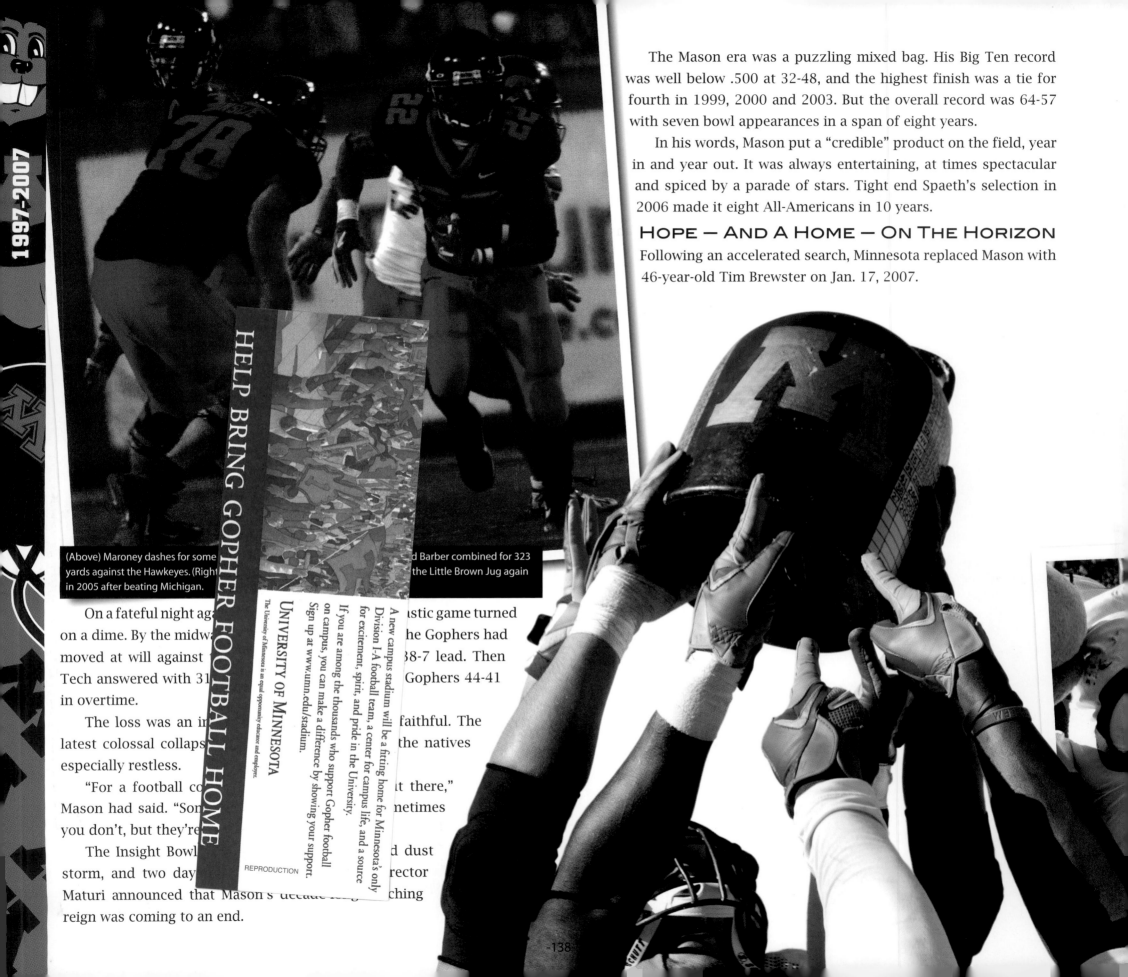

The Mason era was a puzzling mixed bag. His Big Ten record was well below .500 at 32-48, and the highest finish was a tie for fourth in 1999, 2000 and 2003. But the overall record was 64-57 with seven bowl appearances in a span of eight years.

In his words, Mason put a "credible" product on the field, year in and year out. It was always entertaining, at times spectacular and spiced by a parade of stars. Tight end Spaeth's selection in 2006 made it eight All-Americans in 10 years.

HOPE — AND A HOME — ON THE HORIZON

Following an accelerated search, Minnesota replaced Mason with 46-year-old Tim Brewster on Jan. 17, 2007.

(Above) Maroney dashes for some ... yards against the Hawkeyes. (Right ... in 2005 after beating Michigan.

... Barber combined for 323 ... the Little Brown Jug again

On a fateful night ag... on a dime. By the midwa... moved at will against ... Tech answered with 31... in overtime.

The loss was an i... latest colossal collaps... especially restless.

"For a football co... Mason had said. "Son... you don't, but they're...

The Insight Bowl... storm, and two day... Maturi announced that Mason's decade-long ... ching reign was coming to an end.

A new campus stadium will be a fitting home for Minnesota's only Division I-A football team, a center for campus life, and a source for excitement, spirit, and pride in the University.

If you are among the thousands who support Gopher football on campus, you can make a difference by showing your support. Sign up at www.umn.edu/stadium.

UNIVERSITY OF MINNESOTA

The University of Minnesota is an equal opportunity educator and employer.

HELP BRING GOPHER FOOTBALL HOME

REPRODUCTION

...stic game turned ...he Gophers had ...38-7 lead. Then ...Gophers 44-41

...faithful. The ...the natives

...t there," ...netimes

...d dust ...rector

1997-2007

-138-

Brewster had spent the previous five seasons in the National Football League as a tight ends coach for San Diego and Denver. Prior to that, he was an assistant coach on Mack Brown's staffs at North Carolina and at Texas. He built his reputation as a tenacious recruiter and is credited with bringing quarterback Vince Young to the Longhorns.

Brewster also arrived with Rose Bowl experience. As an All-Big Ten tight end, he captained Illinois to the big game against UCLA in 1984.

Since the day he arrived, Brewster has been a fountain of energy, touting the overall strengths of the university and anointing its fans as the "Gopher Nation."

But his first season had more than its share of growing pains, as the Gophers struggled to a 1-11 mark and went winless in the Big Ten. While the offense adjusted to the new spread attack, the defense struggled to hold down opponents.

The low point was a 27-21 loss to North Dakota State, a member of the Football Championship Subdivision (formerly I-AA). The Bison rumbled into

10 BIG GAMES REMEMBERED: 1997-2007

Oct. 8, 2005: Minnesota 23, Michigan 20, in Ann Arbor. It had been 19 years since the Gophers claimed the Little Brown Jug, but the drought ended with a 23-20 upset of the Wolverines in front of 111,117. With time running down and the Gophers facing a third-and-10 on their own 26-yard line, Gary Russell took a handoff and sped 61 yards to the Michigan 13. Three plays later, Jason Giannini nailed a 30-yard field goal with one second remaining for the victory.

(Below) Just when it looked like Minnesota and Michigan were going to go into overtime, the Gophers struck with a long run by Gary Russell and a field goal by Jason Giannini to stun the Wolverines in the final seconds. It was the first time Minnesota had won the jug since 1986, John Gutekunst's first year as coach. (Right) An artist's rendering of TCF Bank Stadium, scheduled to open on campus in 2009.

1997-2007

the Metrodome and trampled the Gophers with 394 yards rushing and 585 total yards.

Despite the most losses in team history, there is hope on the horizon. Freshman quarterback Adam Weber finished with 285 completions, 2,895 passing yards, 24 touchdowns and 3,512 yards of total offense — all single-season team records.

The college football Web site Rivals.com rated Minnesota's 2008 recruiting class the 17th best in the nation, trailing only Ohio State and Michigan in the Big Ten — an extraordinary accomplishment in light of the 1-11 season. Sam Maresh, a highly rated local player, is staying home, as is Ryan Grant, grandson of former Gopher and NFL coaching icon Bud Grant.

Perhaps more importantly, the return of football to the Minnesota campus is just around the corner. On April 7, 2008, 100-year-old Hilding Mortenson laid the first brick of a new stadium — a poetic act given that he worked on Memorial Stadium as a high school sophomore in 1924. He told me he can still picture Bruce Smith running through the mud on his 80-yard gallop against Michigan in 1940.

The Gophers will kick it off in the new stadium against Air Force on Sept. 12, 2009. Brewster predicts there will be magic in the new stadium and not a dry eye in the house for the opener.

As fans are blinking away the tears, they might conjure up images of the legends who roamed Memorial Stadium and Northrop Field in decades past: Pilly and Pug, Biggie and Bronko, Bernie and Bruce, Sandy and Bobby.

There will be magic, indeed, and a new generation of Golden Gopher memories.

10 BIG GAMES REMEMBERED: 1997-2007

Dec. 29, 2006: Texas Tech 44, Minnesota 41, in Tempe. Minnesota appeared to be well on its way to an Insight Bowl victory. Midway through the third quarter, the Gophers had built a 38-7 lead on touchdowns by Jack Simmons, Amir Pinnix, Justin Valentine, Ernie Wheelright and Logan Payne. But Texas Tech reeled off 31 points in a row to send the game to overtime, and answered Minnesota's field goal with a touchdown for the victory. It was the largest comeback ever in a bowl.

(Left) Center Greg Eslinger is one of the most decorated Minnesota linemen ever — two-time All-American, two-time Academic All-American and winner of both the Rimington and Outland trophies. He was drafted by the Denver Broncos in 2006. (Inset) Tim Brewster became Minnesota's head coach on Jan. 17, 2007. (Opposite page) The new stadium will bring the Gophers back to the campus and conjure up memories of the past glory days. The big opener is Sept. 12, 2009, against Air Force.

TCF BANK STADIUM™

TCF BANK STADIUM

1997-2007

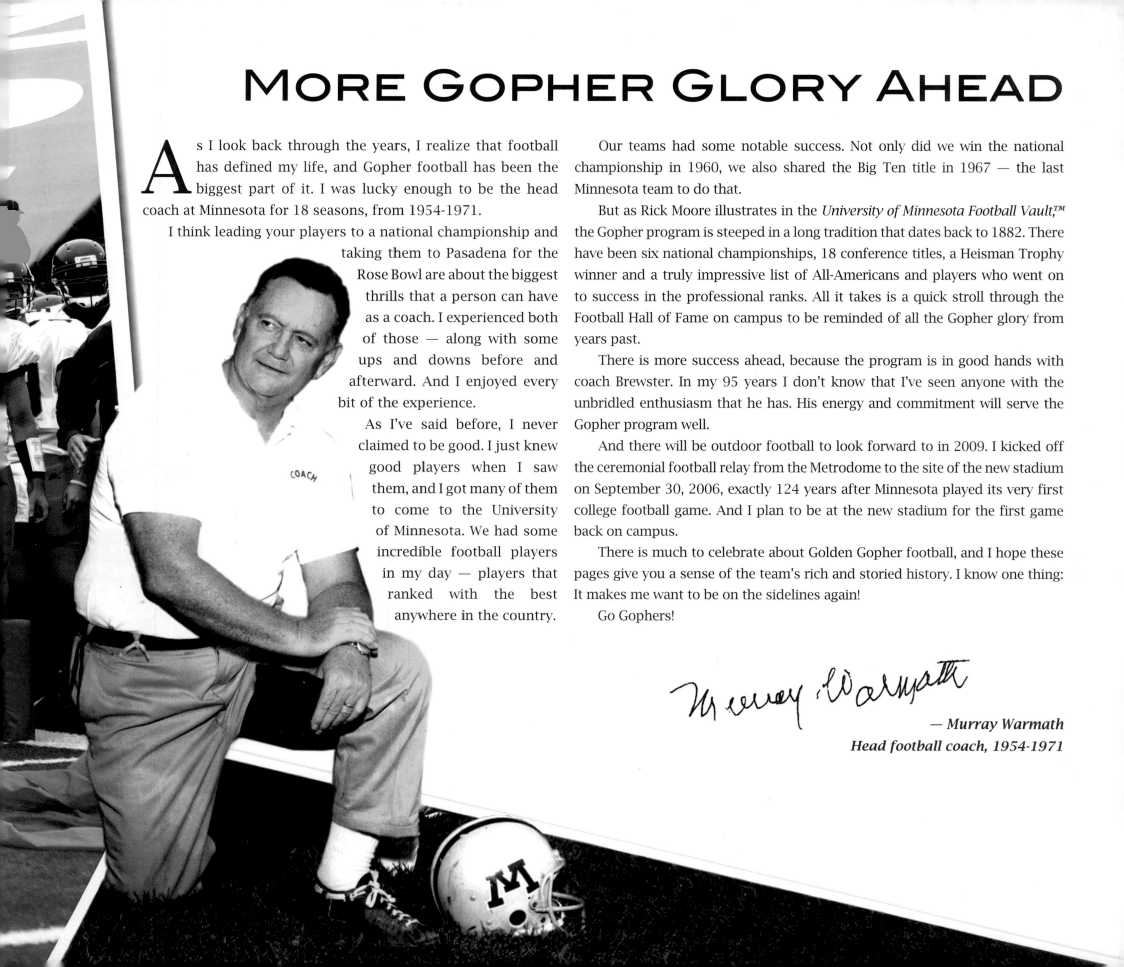

MORE GOPHER GLORY AHEAD

As I look back through the years, I realize that football has defined my life, and Gopher football has been the biggest part of it. I was lucky enough to be the head coach at Minnesota for 18 seasons, from 1954-1971.

I think leading your players to a national championship and taking them to Pasadena for the Rose Bowl are about the biggest thrills that a person can have as a coach. I experienced both of those — along with some ups and downs before and afterward. And I enjoyed every bit of the experience.

As I've said before, I never claimed to be good. I just knew good players when I saw them, and I got many of them to come to the University of Minnesota. We had some incredible football players in my day — players that ranked with the best anywhere in the country.

Our teams had some notable success. Not only did we win the national championship in 1960, we also shared the Big Ten title in 1967 — the last Minnesota team to do that.

But as Rick Moore illustrates in the *University of Minnesota Football Vault,*™ the Gopher program is steeped in a long tradition that dates back to 1882. There have been six national championships, 18 conference titles, a Heisman Trophy winner and a truly impressive list of All-Americans and players who went on to success in the professional ranks. All it takes is a quick stroll through the Football Hall of Fame on campus to be reminded of all the Gopher glory from years past.

There is more success ahead, because the program is in good hands with coach Brewster. In my 95 years I don't know that I've seen anyone with the unbridled enthusiasm that he has. His energy and commitment will serve the Gopher program well.

And there will be outdoor football to look forward to in 2009. I kicked off the ceremonial football relay from the Metrodome to the site of the new stadium on September 30, 2006, exactly 124 years after Minnesota played its very first college football game. And I plan to be at the new stadium for the first game back on campus.

There is much to celebrate about Golden Gopher football, and I hope these pages give you a sense of the team's rich and storied history. I know one thing: It makes me want to be on the sidelines again!

Go Gophers!

— Murray Warmath
Head football coach, 1954-1971

ABOUT THE AUTHOR

Rick Moore has spent most of his life in the Gopher State. He grew up in St. Paul and graduated from Forest Lake High School, where he played football, basketball and baseball, and even attended a Cal Stoll football passing camp. In college he shifted his focus from athletics to writing and earned a B.A. in print journalism from the University of St. Thomas.

Following several years of leading adventure camping tours throughout North America and a stint coordinating service-learning programs in South Dakota, Moore began working at the University of Minnesota in 1999. For the past five years he has been a senior editor in the Office of University Relations.

Over the years, Moore's articles have appeared in more than 20 publications, including two books. This is his first full-length book, and he is proud to have had a hand in chronicling a team with such a rich and storied tradition. He is also anxious to watch outdoor football again soon.

ACKNOWLEDGMENTS

First and foremost, much love to my family: to my amazing father (like Sandy Stephens, a native of Uniontown, Pennsylvania), who instilled in me a love of the game and at least a fraction of his work ethic; to my loving and nurturing mother, who has always supported me as I followed my bliss; and to my sister, Pat, and brother, Tom, and their families, who continue to inspire me.

Special thanks to Lois Hendrickson, Elisabeth Kaplan and Karen Klinkenberg at the University of Minnesota Archives for shepherding me through the vast stores of invaluable information on the early days of Gopher football — the boxes of clips, game programs, scrapbooks, etc. — and to Tom Wistrcill, Garry Bowman and Jeff Keiser in the Athletics Department for their assistance with this project.

In addition to the books cited, I drew heavily upon newspaper accounts of the games of yesteryear. After many hours reading old clippings and microfilm, I gained a new appreciation for the rich writing that sucked me into the world of sports as a youth.

To all my friends, to my terrific colleagues in University Relations, to Uncle Ed for his ticket stub and stories from the 1962 Rose Bowl, and to the mostly patient Minnesota football fans who are ready to be roused again: Go Gophers!

BIBLIOGRAPHY

• Gray, James. *The University of Minnesota: 1851-1951*. Minneapolis, MN: University of Minnesota Press, 1951.
• Rainbolt, Richard. *Gold Glory*. Wayzata, MN: Turtinen Publishing Co., 1972.
• Turtinen, Ralph, ed. *100 Years of Golden Gopher Football*. Minneapolis, MN: Men's Intercollegiate Athletic Department of the University of Minnesota, 1981.
• Christensen, Ray. *Ray Christensen's Gopher Tales: Stories from All Eleven University of Minnesota's Men's Sports*. Champaign, IL: Sports Publishing, 2002.
• Rippel, Joel A. *Game of My Life: Minnesota (Memorable Stories of Gophers Football)*. Champaign, IL: Sports Publishing, 2007.
• Brady, Tim. *Gopher Gold: Legendary Figures, Brilliant Blunders, and Amazing Feats at the University of Minnesota*. St. Paul, MN: Minnesota Historical Society Press, 2007.
• Bernstein, Ross. *Pigskin Pride: Celebrating a Century of Minnesota Football*. Minneapolis, MN: Nodin Press, 2000.
• Papas, Al Jr. *Gopher Sketchbook*. Minneapolis, MN: Nodin Press, 1990.
• Quirk, James P. *Minnesota Football: The Golden Years 1932-1941*. Self-published, 1984.
• McCallum, John D. *Big Ten Football Since 1895*. Radnor, PA: Chilton Book Company, 1976.
• *Football at Minnesota: The Story of Thirty Years' Contests on the Gridiron* (The *Minnesota Alumni Weekly*, 11-9-14, Vol. XIV, No. 9), Published by The General Alumni Association of the University of Minnesota, 1914.
• University of Minnesota game programs and media guides, 1898-2007.
• Gophersports.com: *http://gophersports.com*; UMNnews: *http://umn.edu/umnnews*; Rivals.com: *http://rivals.com*. (Accessed January-April 2008).

DIGITAL IMAGES PROVIDED BY UNIVERSITY OF MINNESOTA ARCHIVES, MINNEAPOLIS

UNIVERSITY OF MINNESOTA™

ALL-TIME LEADERS

Career Rushing Yards Top 15

1.	Darrell Thompson	4,654
2.	Laurence Maroney	3,933
3.	Thomas Hamner	3,810
4.	Marion Barber III	3,276
5.	Chris Darkins	3,235
6.	Marion Barber Jr.	3,094
7.	Tellis Redmon	2,481
8.	Amir Pinnix	2,439
9.	Garry White	2,353
10.	Pug Lund	2,264
11.	Paul Giel	2,188
12.	Rickey Foggie	2,150
13.	Red Williams	1,999
14.	Thomas Tapeh	1,958
15.	Herb Joesting	1,850

Career Passing Yards Top 15

1.	Bryan Cupito	7,446
2.	Cory Sauter	6,834
3.	Asad Abdul-Khaliq	6,660
4.	Marquel Fleetwood	5,279
5.	Rickey Foggie	5,162
6.	Mike Hohensee	4,792
7.	Tim Schade	3,986
8.	Tony Dungy	3,515
9.	Billy Cockerham	3,483
10.	Scott Schaffner	3,472
11.	Mark Carlson	3,128
12.	Craig Curry	3,061
13.	Adam Weber	2,895
14.	Travis Cole	2,747
15.	John Hankinson	2,561

Career Receiving Yards Top 15

1.	Ron Johnson	2,989
2.	Tutu Atwell	2,640
3.	Ernie Wheelwright	2,434
4.	Ryan Thelwell	2,232
5.	Jared Ellerson	2,054
6.	Luke Leverson	1,843
7.	Omar Douglas	1,681
8.	Dwayne McMullen	1,627
9.	Aaron Osterman	1,598
10.	Aaron Hosack	1,463
11.	Logan Payne	1,344
12.	Chester Cooper	1,317
13.	Matt Spaeth	1,293
14.	Eric Decker	1,287
15.	Elmer Bailey	1,266

Career Scoring Top 15

1.	Dan Nystrom	367
2.	Chip Lohmiller	268
3.	Darrell Thompson	262
4.	Marion Barber Jr.	218
(Tie)	Paul Rogind	218
6.	Jim Gallery	216
7.	Marion Barber III	210
8.	Mike Chalberg	208
9.	Laurence Maroney	204
10.	Ron Johnson	186
11.	Rhys Lloyd	180
12.	Adam Bailey	179
13.	Brent Berglund	175
14.	Chris Darkins	156
(Tie)	Rickey Foggie	156